MAJORS

by Dr. Randy T. Johnson

WITH CONTRIBUTIONS BY:

NOBLE BAIRD	MICHAEL FOX
PAT BEDELL	RICHIE HENSON
HOLLY BOSTON	KENNY HOVIS
JOHN CARTER	JOHN HUBBARD
JAMES CLOUSE	DEBBIE KERR
CALEB COMBS	JOSH LAHRING
ISAIAH COMBS	CHUCK LINDSEY
JAYSON COMBS	JAMES MANN
JOSHUA COMBS	KEN PERRY
SIERRA COMBS	RYAN STORY
MATTHEW DARDEN	HOLLY WELLS
DONNA FOX	TOMMY YOUNGQUIST

DESIGNED BY: CASEY MAXWELL
FORMATTED BY: SHAWNA JOHNSON

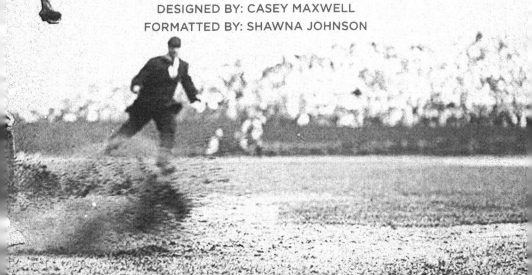

Copyright © 2018 The River Church

All rights reserved. No part of this book may be reproduced or transmitted in any form or by any means, electronic or mechanical, including photocopying, recording or by any information storage and retrieval system, without the written permission of The River Church. Inquiries should be sent to the publisher.

First Edition, July 2018

Published by:
The River Church
8393 E. Holly Rd.
Holly, MI 48442

Scriptures are taken from the Bible,
English Standard Version (ESV)

THE RIVER CHURCH

Printed in the United States of America

CONTENTS

REACH

WEEK 1

11   Study Guide

17   Devotion 1: Ramblings of the Redeemed

21   Devotion 2: My Story

25   Devotion 3: God is in the Seasons

29   Devotion 4: Loving the Community

31   Devotion 5: Go!

33   Devotion 6: Serving

GROW

WEEK 3

59   Study Guide

67   Devotion 1: Milk, Meat, and Apples

69   Devotion 2: Growth Takes Time

71   Devotion 3: The Path to the Prize

75   Devotion 4: Intentional

77   Devotion 5: Spiritual Growth

81   Devotion 6: Starting Strong

GATHER

WEEK 2

37   Study Guide

43   Devotion 1: No Longer Slaves

45   Devotion 2: In the Presence of Jehovah

49   Devotion 3: The Lamb of God

51   Devotion 4: Revelation Song

53   Devotion 5: Great are You, Lord

55   Devotion 6: O Praise the Name

INERRANCY OF SCRIPTURE

WEEK 4

85   Study Guide

93   Devotion 1: 2 Timothy 3:16-17

97   Devotion 2: 2 Peter 1:20-21

99   Devotion 3: 1 Thessalonians 2:13

103   Devotion 4: John 17:17

105   Devotion 5: Isaiah 40:8

107   Devotion 6: Matthew 5:18

SALVATION BY FAITH & GRACE OF GOD

WEEK 5

111 Study Guide

117 Devotion 1: John 1:12

119 Devotion 2: 1 John 5:5

121 Devotion 3: Romans 3:20-24

123 Devotion 4: John 3:16

125 Devotion 5: 1 John 5:11-13

129 Devotion 6: Ephesians 2:8-10

TRINITY

WEEK 6

133 Study Guide

139 Devotion 1: Matthew 3:16-17

141 Devotion 2: Colossians 2:9

143 Devotion 3: Matthew 28:19

145 Devotion 4: 2 Corinthians 13:14

147 Devotion 5: Matthew 1:23

151 Devotion 6: John 1:1

JESUS IS GOD

WEEK 7

155 Study Guide

163 Devotion 1: John 1:1

165 Devotion 2: Exodus 3:14 & John 8:58

167 Devotion 3: Philippians 2:5-8

171 Devotion 4: John 10:30-33

173 Devotion 5: Isaiah 9:6

175 Devotion 6: John 20:28

JESUS WAS SINLESS

WEEK 8

179 Study Guide

187 Devotion 1: John 19:4

189 Devotion 2: 1 Peter 1:18-19

191 Devotion 3: 1 Peter 2:22

193 Devotion 4: 1 John 3:5

195 Devotion 5: 2 Corinthians 5:21

199 Devotion 6: Hebrews 4:15

CONTENTS

JESUS DIED FOR OUR SINS

WEEK 9

203 Study Guide

209 Devotion 1: Romans 3:10-12

211 Devotion 2: Romans 3:23

213 Devotion 3: Colossians 2:13-14

215 Devotion 4: Galatians 5:17

219 Devotion 5: Jeremiah 17:9

221 Devotion 6: Ecclesiastes 7:20

THE RETURN OF CHRIST

WEEK 11

253 Study Guide

259 Devotion 1: Matthew 24:44-45

261 Devotion 2: Luke 12:35-38

263 Devotion 3: 2 Peter 3:10-18

265 Devotion 4: Revelation 22:20-21

269 Devotion 5: 1 Thessalonians 4:13-18

273 Devotion 6: Matthew 25:13

JESUS ROSE AGAIN & THE ASCENSION

WEEK 10

225 Study Guide

233 Devotion 1: 1 Thessalonians 4:14

235 Devotion 2: Mark 16:1-6

237 Devotion 3: Luke 24:5-7

241 Devotion 4: John 20:24-29

245 Devotion 5: 1 Corinthians 15:3-8

249 Devotion 6: Acts 1:3

HELL & HEAVEN

WEEK 12

277 Study Guide

285 Devotion 1:Revelation 14:10-11

287 Devotion 2: John 3:16

289 Devotion 3: John 3:36

291 Devotion 4: Revelation 21:8

295 Devotion 5: Romans 2:6-8

299 Devotion 6: Matthew 25:46

8

PREFACE

Everyone has a belief system, philosophy, and worldview. The real challenge is not necessarily what people believe, but why they believe what they believe. Too many "Christians" fall away from what they were taught because they never stopped to find support material. They do not know how to explain or defend their view. They actually do not know how to support their core values.

Majors consists of twelve study guides to address the "major" essential aspects of Christianity. These are written for personal or group discussion. There are also seventy-two devotions that dig deeper into the Bible so you can know why you know what you know.

Majors was written for two main reasons. First, it is designed to help those who are searching to better understand the foundations of Christianity. Second, *Majors* targets those who are followers of Jesus Christ who want to better understand what the Bible has to say concerning their worldview.

One of the biggest tragedies in America today is that we send our children off to college and the world without them knowing why they believe what they have professed.

01

REACH

JAYSON COMBS,
FAMILY PASTOR

LESSON ONE REACH

My father grew up in a crazy home. His father died when he was seven when a coal-mine collapsed on him. At that time, my dad moved to Michigan with his mother and siblings. My grandmother then got remarried to a man named Nevil. Every time I hear this man's name brought up, the overwhelming sentiment is that he was one bad dude. He had spent time in prison and did some pretty wicked things. My father's crazy life continued until he was 33. He then accepted Jesus Christ as his Lord and Savior and everything changed in his life. There was this fire in my dad that he wanted people to come to know Jesus. This fire was not just a little fire inside of him; it was a huge fire!

The marriage between my grandmother and Nevil did not last very long. Just recently my father told me a crazy story. He told me that one day he drove to Kentucky because he wanted to witness to his former stepfather. He wanted to see if that man would come to know Jesus Christ as his Lord and Savior. Even though he did all those horrible things to my father and grandmother, my father had such a fire inside of him to be a witness for Jesus.

Do you know anyone that has that fire inside of them? What would lead someone to do something like that?

Passion

Zeal

On a scale of 1-10, how hot do you think your fire burns to witness for Jesus? Explain.

Philippians 1:12-14 says, ***"I want you to know, brothers, that what has happened to me has really served to advance the gospel, so***

LESSON ONE REACH

that it has become known throughout the whole imperial guard and to all the rest that my imprisonment is for Christ. And most of the brothers, having become confident in the Lord by my imprisonment, are much more bold to speak the word without fear." See Acts 27+28

Do you know where Paul was while he is writing this? What does he tell us is happening?

this

How does Paul desire to spread the Word according to verses 14?

thru the family of God

How can we get better at reaching people?

Philippians 1:9-11 adds, *"And it is my prayer that your love may abound more and more, with knowledge and all discernment, so that you may approve what is excellent, and so be pure and blameless for the day of Christ, filled with the fruit of righteousness that comes through Jesus Christ, to the glory and praise of God."*

I believe Paul prayed this prayer for his friends because this is what filled him.

LESSON ONE REACH

What things are we called to have as follows of Christ according to this passage?

Knowledge ; Discernment

How do you think these things translate into being able to reach people for Jesus? _If Our life matches our message then we will reach people. Phill. /27_

There are three things that I think we must get better at if we are going to be better at reaching people for Christ.

1. Connect with people

I will never forget walking into a restaurant with one of my pastor friends. We had not seen each other for a few years as he had moved to Texas. As we went to order our food, the lady who was taking our order had tattoos down her arms and bunny rabbit ears on her head (side note: I have got nothing against either). My pastor friend instantly connected with her. His questions made her feel like he was someone she could trust. Just in a matter of seconds, I watched a total stranger open up and feel welcomed.

Have you ever seen someone who was able to do this?

"Let your life be worthy of the gospel."

LESSON ONE REACH

How can we learn to ask good questions? What are some situations you could use in a better way?

_____

_____

_____

2. Care for people

When Paul says in verse 9 *"that your love may abound more and more,"* this is what I think he is addressing. We need to learn to love people better. We need to love people in the church and people outside of the church.

When was the last time you stepped out of your comfort zone to love someone (co-worker, neighbor, or teammate)?

_____

_____

_____

What holds you back from doing this?

_____

_____

_____

3. Communicate the Truth

In verse 9, Paul says that we need to love with knowledge and discernment. Giving truth takes wisdom. We need to have knowledge about God's Word and discernment on how to give it.

LESSON ONE REACH

Does leading someone to the Lord make you nervous? What are some keys verses to use when telling someone about how to accept Christ as their Savior?

John 3:16
Romans 3:23 (Romans Road)
" 5:8
" 6:23
" 10:9

Memorize

As a small group, I challenge you to step out of your box this week in at least one of these areas. Come back next week and share your experience.

Read this week:

• Eph. 4:15 "Speaking the truth in love"

• 1 Peter 3:15 "this being prepared for the reason of the hope that is in you."

• Matthew 25: Why we go into prisons

15

LESSON ONE REACH

RAMBLINGS OF THE REDEEMED

REACH, DEVOTION 1
Matthew Darden | *Custodial*

Born the second of five to two Crystal Meth addict parents in rural Missouri, my childhood was filled with CPS visits, drawn-out stays with relatives, and the always changing environment of houses due to the nature of the drug world. The cycles mentioned above continued until I was eight years old when my dad was in prison. My aunt from Michigan came down to take him to a halfway house. In the time before he had to check in, he and his sister came to visit my mom and us kids. Upon arriving, he saw that the six of us plus one of my mother's friends are all staying in a two-bed motel room. My aunt offered to bring us up to Michigan for a vacation to give my mom a chance to get her stuff together a little bit. Two days into our Michigan trip my mother was arrested. With both parents incarcerated and us kids away from our usual relatives, we stayed with my aunt who opened her home to us kids and began to take care of us.

I began to experience love and consistency of life I had never been exposed to before; I flourished. During these next six years, while I lived at my aunt's house, I became active in church, received Christ, and served in various capacities while furthering my faith. As I entered the last year of my middle school career, I moved in with my dad and became entranced with the world and "all it had to offer." Doubts crept in, and I began to question my faith. My dad was now clean from Meth but was still a very heavy smoker and not very interested in parenting. This lack of parental supervision encouraged me to explore my various lustful desires. The continued strain on the relationship between my father and I, in addition to his alcoholic new bride, caused me to move out when I was sixteen.

REACH DEVOTION 1

I stayed with friends until the end of the school year, then having reconnected with my mother returned to Missouri under the pretense of her being clean. Within days I saw that she was not clean; this discouragement and bitterness allowed me to let go of any previous reservations I had, and I lived completely for myself and any fickle desire that presented itself to me. I returned to my maternal aunt's house for the remainder of high school and beginning of college.

For the next three years, I partied and doubted attempting to satisfy that which is insatiable. In bitterness, I looked to the world for freedom; in brokenness, I found all-encompassing chains. To serve a master that is never pleased or satisfied is a horrible thing indeed. By the end of these three years, my mother's hepatitis B had become liver cirrhosis. Abandoned by who she thought held her dear, that is her friends and lovers in the drug world, she had nobody. A good friend and I moved in to help her. At this point, having found no contentment in all the things I felt would surely give my life meaning or at the very least happiness, I began to think about my faith a little more. My mother's sickness progressed until she finally passed. Throughout my mother's sickness, I prayed occasionally but never one time for healing, rather for salvation for her soul.

The seed planted when I was yet a child, remained there no matter what substance or alcohol I dumped on it. That seed continued to convict me and draw me closer. My mother's death shook me up, and made me evaluate my morality and what I would leave behind when I passed. The question became how do I want to live my life? I began for the first time to get into the Word for myself. I was enthralled, captivated, and astounded by the realness and applications that the Bible showed me. Having been saved as a child, at age nineteen, I began to live for God. What did I receive? Contentment, forgiveness, a purpose, and peace that surpasses all understanding were part of the gift.

My favorite verse is Titus 3:3-5 (KJV), *"For we ourselves also were sometimes foolish, disobedient, deceived, serving divers lusts and pleasures, living in malice and envy, hateful and hating one another. But after that the kindness and love of God our Savior toward man appeared, not by works of righteousness which we have done, but according to his mercy he saved us, by the washing of regeneration, and the renewing of the Holy Ghost."*

REACH DEVOTION 1

MY STORY

REACH, DEVOTION 2
Pat Bedell | *Special Projects*

I am a sinner. I am not perfect. I will never be worthy. However, I am a child of God, and that is the greatest blessing I have never deserved.

I grew up in a small town in a somewhat sheltered home life. It was not that my parents did not necessarily trust me, but they also did not want to expose me to the negativity of the world. I grew up in a Catholic church going sporadically over the course of my youth. When I started high school, I became a little more interested in God and decided to attend more often. After graduation and heading off to college, I found myself with a small void, but I did not take the initiative to seek out God in my first year of college.

I grew up in a wonderful household. My dad is the hardest worker I know, and he taught me about work ethic, sacrifices, and how to love with everything you have. My mother is the most thoughtful person I know. She taught me to think of others before yourself, and to be the kindest person in the room. They taught me many other positive things while growing up, but the negative things in my head were brewing with every compliment I ever received. Pride was my kryptonite, and it always struck hard. I was great in sports, a phenomenal musician, and was good at just about anything I tried. I was "that guy" that was good at everything. Many thought it was cool, many despised my talents. There were occasions it was hard to get my head through the door. I was always looked up to by my family to set a good example and to be a positive role model for my younger siblings and cousins. After having such a prideful attitude

REACH DEVOTION 2

for myself, I somewhat felt pressured by family to keep up with the pride to make sure that my kin would follow suit. I was headed down a path that only would lead to selfishness and boastfulness which is what took over my life in my first year of college.

My second year of college is when a new friend of mine invited me to an on-campus ministry. He told me it was non-denominational which did not mean much to me at the time, but it opened my eyes the moment the gathering had started. My first thought was "there are drums in church?" From then after that, I became more interested in God. It was late October of 2007 when I gave my life to Christ. I felt such a burden lifted off of my shoulders from all of life's hardships. It was then that I learned that no matter what I was going through, I could let God handle everything in my life. I started to learn more stories in the Bible, and there was a sermon taught to me about pride, boasting, and selfishness. It hit me pretty hard, and it was then that I learned that pride is the work of Satan and that I should only boast in the name of Jesus. I also was challenged that I should put others before myself as my mother taught me and what the Word of Jesus tells us to do.

After being baptized and living my life for Jesus, I began to use my talents in a peculiar way. I played music for the worship team, I would play intramural sports with a team affiliated with the Christian organization (knowing we were going to lose pretty bad), and I would use my trade skills to help those in need on mission trips. It was not long after that I was taught out of the book of Matthew about the parable of talents. Matthew 25: 14-30 states, *"For it will be like a man going on a journey, who called his servants and entrusted to them his property. To one he gave five talents, to another two, to another one, to each according to his ability. Then he went away. He who had received the five talents went at once and traded with them, and he made five talents more.*

REACH DEVOTION 2

So also he who had the two talents made two talents more. But he who had received the one talent went and dug into the ground and hid his master's money. Now after a long time, the master of those servants came and settled accounts with them. And he who had received the five talents came forward, bringing five talents more, saying, 'Master, you delivered to me five talents; here, I have made five talents more.' His master said to him, 'Well done, good and faithful servant. You have been faithful over a little; I will set you over much. Enter into the joy of your master.' And he also who had the two talents came forward, saying, 'Master, you delivered to me two talents; here, I have made two talents more.' His master said to him, 'Well done, good and faithful servant. You have been faithful over a little; I will set you over much. Enter into the joy of your master.' He also who had received the one talent came forward, saying, 'Master, I knew you to be a hard man, reaping where you did not sow, and gathering where you scattered no seed, so I was afraid, and I went and hid your talent in the ground. Here, you have what is yours.' But his master answered him, 'You wicked and slothful servant! You knew that I reap where I have not sown and gather where I scattered no seed? Then you ought to have invested my money with the bankers, and at my coming I should have received what was my own with interest. So take the talent from him and give it to him who has the ten talents. For to everyone who has will more be given, and he will have an abundance. But from the one who has not, even what he has will be taken away. And cast the worthless servant into the outer darkness. In that place there will be weeping and gnashing of teeth.'"

After reading this parable, I knew how to use my talents to glorify God. I was going to use my talents to spread the Gospel of Jesus. Since then, my talents seem to be growing in number, and I will turn around and use them for His glory. I feel it is such a blessing and honor to be able to be a servant in His kingdom.

With a wife of three years and our first child on the way, I am so excited to be able to bring our child up with the love of Christ in his or her life. With this new adventure, we are about to embrace, putting God at the center of our household and with steadfast prayer, I believe God is going to bless our home abundantly!

GOD IS IN THE SEASONS

REACH, DEVOTION 3
Kenny Hovis | *Prison Ministry Director*

I love living in Michigan. I have been to many other beautiful cities, states, and even countries. Many of them are known for their beautiful waters or mountains. So, why is it that I am so enamored with this magnificent state? For me, it is the four seasons and what each of them has to offer. First, there is the freshness of the air on a winter morning! Spring brings the fragrance of newly blooming flowers. Hours spent on any one of a thousand lakes or Great Lakes, swimming, boating, or just enjoying a picturesque sunset is nearby during the summer. Finally, there is the grand majesty of fall with its wildly diverse color, each one separate, but together forming a masterpiece by the original art Master. Yes, God is in the seasons.

Through the years of my life, there have been different seasons. I have served in many capacities in the church. I sang in the choir, traveled in a singing group, taught Sunday school, was a youth director, served in jail ministry, and led worship. I even felt God was leading me to go to school to become a youth pastor. All the while I told myself that I was doing it for God, but as I look back now, I realize that I was more interested in the approval and praise of men. I was trying to earn my way to Heaven. I yearned to have people like me think I had it all together.

While I was spending so much time trying to earn my way into God's graces, I was neglecting my family. My wife grew resentful of my time away, and we grew apart. I convinced myself I was the one being wronged, and I stood defiant to all that the Holy Spirit was convicting me. As a result, my marriage of 20 years ended.

REACH DEVOTION 3

Jeremiah 50:31-32 says, *"Behold, I am against you, O proud one, declares the Lord God of Hosts, for your day has come, the time when I will punish you. The proud one shall stumble and fall, with none to raise him up, and I will kindle fire in his cities, and it will devour all that is around him."*

I went into a dark season in my life and spent some time trying to convince myself, family, and friends that I had been wronged. The great deceiver had convinced me that my actions were just, and that all would be fine. My faith waned, and I blamed God. Through this season, I reached my lowest point and realized I could not fix it. I had disqualified myself from being a pastor, but if nothing else, I wanted my faith in God to be more real to me than ever. I still pray that prayer today.

Ephesians 2:8-10 is so clear and powerful, *"For by grace you have been saved through faith. And this is not your own doing; it is the gift of God, not a result of works, so that no one may boast. For we are his workmanship, created in Christ Jesus for good works, which God prepared beforehand, that we should walk in them."*

The season of my life since then has been a constant struggle for me to not feel like damaged goods. I have a nagging voice that chirps in my ear saying, "You are useless to God." God's desire through eternity, even to the point of sacrificing His Son, is to have a restored relationship with His creation. I believe God is in the restoration business. He restores us to Himself when we are repentant children, which enables Him to bless us again.

I have been married to a wonderful woman for 13 years now. I see her living out her faith, God revealing Himself to her, and her faith becoming more real to her every day. Now we still struggle to find the courage to deny ourselves, and live by faith daily, but it is our goal. We pray that we are an example to our children of how to live by faith.

Now, I tell that voice that I have a purpose. I have been restored by the work of Christ on the cross to a faith, stronger now more than ever. God still has a plan for me.

REACH DEVOTION 3

LOVING THE COMMUNITY

REACH, DEVOTION 4
Noble Baird | *Community Center Director*

Several months ago, I received a phone call from a friend who attends the church, and he told me that there was someone in need of help from the Community Center. I asked him what time he could bring the man out and he said they would be at the center by 4:00 pm. So, I went to the center early, told Miss Pat the situation, and we gathered together a couple of boxes of items that we thought the man would need. Once four o'clock rolled around, my friend walked into the center with the man who I had been on the phone with earlier; that is when I had the privilege of watching God work.

In 1 Corinthians, Paul writes about the Body of Christ, which is the culmination of us as followers of Christ. He writes about this to explain how every believer plays an essential role in the Church. In 1 Corinthians 12:12-20, he writes, *"For just as the body is one and has many members, and all the members of the body, though many, are one body, so it is with Christ. For in one Spirit we were all baptized into one body—Jews or Greeks, slaves or free—and all were made to drink of one Spirit. For the body does not consist of one member but of many. If the foot should say, 'Because I am not a hand, I do not belong to the body,' that would not make it any less a part of the body. And if the ear should say, 'Because I am not an eye, I do not belong to the body,' that would not make it any less a part of the body. If the whole body were an eye, where would be the sense of hearing? If the whole body were an ear, where would be the sense of smell? But as it is, God arranged the members in*

REACH DEVOTION 4

the body, each one of them, as he chose. If all were a single member, where would the body be? As it is, there are many parts, yet one body." It is within this passage, that Paul explains the appearance of the Church. Often people will affiliate themselves with one specific denomination or even get wrapped up following one preacher. However, Paul writes to the church in Corinth and us, explaining how there is no separation and how we are all united in one body in Him.

As Miss Pat showed the man all that we had for him and his family, I saw tears start to run down the man's face. He was speechless at the fact that a church that he did not associate with, nor had he ever stepped foot in, met him with open arms. All of the items that we were able to give to this man was from all of you, the Church. At the Community Center, all we have is donated. The clothing, bread, dishes, towels, blankets, and small household appliances are used to touch lives because of what you gave. That afternoon, a man's life was changed, and he experienced the love of Christ through the body of Christ working together to show him and his amazing family love. So, thank you Church. Thank you for being a family and coming together, as the body of Christ, to love those in our community who are in need of His love!

GO!

REACH, DEVOTION 5
Noble Baird | *Community Center Director*

Over the past couple years, I have had the privilege of stepping foot in prison yards all over Ohio. If you had asked me when I was in high school if I would ever visit a prison, I would have told you that you were crazy! However, after my first time going in with the team, God truly placed a need in my heart. All throughout my college career at Moody, I had heard of various prison ministries and even had opportunities to go to Cook County Jail in downtown Chicago. I was always hesitant because I had no idea how I could ever relate, greet, let alone begin a conversation with someone who was in prison. Honestly, I was scared.

In Matthew 25: 24-40, Jesus gives a list of physical needs which had been supplemented unknowingly by those who are followers of Christ. In verse 36, He says, *"I was naked and you clothed me, I was sick and you visited me, I was in prison and you came to me."* Within this passage, Jesus is giving us a clear and tangible picture of what it looks like to meet the physical needs of the lost. In this case, He very clearly mentions those who are in prison. He does not stop there. He ends this passage by saying in verse 40, *"Truly, I say to you, as you did it to one of the least of these my brothers, you did it to me."* Jesus tells us plain and simple that when we visited the lost and broken in prison, we are doing it for His glory.

Back in the summer of 2016, I went to Noble Correctional Institute for the first time (maybe a little biased, but this is always my favorite prison to visit). After we had finished playing our set and Pastor Jim finished his message; we had the opportunity to talk and pray

REACH DEVOTION 5

with the inmates. I was quickly approached by a man named Trey and his friend who noticed my ridiculous faces I made while playing drums and they wanted to talk. Although we only had a few minutes together, I was able to hear their stories, and they both eagerly asked me for prayer. This past year in 2017, I was able to return to NCI. While I was playing, I looked out as we had over 1,300 inmates gathered around and sure enough there in the front I saw my friend Trey. When it came time for us to talk and pray with the inmates again, Trey ran over to me and gave me a big hug telling me all that had happened this past year.

I honestly have no idea where Trey is today, if all went according to plan, he is reunited with his wife and his little girl, Layla. No matter, I do know one thing for sure, it is that Trey knows Jesus as His Savior. I have never forgotten Trey, and even though I doubt I will ever see him again during my time here on earth, I am excited to know that we will one day be reunited in the presence of our Savior and I cannot wait to get another big hug from him! So, my challenge is simple, GO! Jesus calls us in Matthew 28:19, *"Go therefore and make disciples."* The only way to reach the lost is to get up, get out of our comfort zone, and GO!

SERVING

REACH, DEVOTION 6
Noble Baird | *Community Center Director*

For many years, serving was always on my list of weekly to-do's, and I was always able to mark it off on Sunday mornings. Every Sunday for a majority of my middle school and high school years, I would find myself back in children's church with my parents or Pastor Bonnie. You see, I honestly had no desire to sit in "big church" or listen to the pastor's preaching, it just was not very fun. So, I asked Pastor Bonnie and my parents if I could help out in the children's ministry and they allowed it. As I was escaping the big church and checking off my assumed "serving" box every week, I was missing the point.

Paul writes in Colossians chapter 3 about this concept of serving. However, he turns the tables and writes to us about it in a new light. In Colossians 3:23-24 he writes, *"Whatever you do, work heartily, as for the Lord and not for men, knowing that from the Lord you will receive the inheritance as your reward. You are serving the Lord Christ."* I am not sure if it can be said any clearer or more simple. Paul reminds us as followers of Christ that in whatever capacity we are serving, we must remember the One we are doing it for, Christ.

Although for years I was stuck in the mindset of simply checking off a box, I am so thankful for the words that Paul wrote. It reminded me of the need to serve not simply to check off a box, but because of the One I was serving. I know at times it can be difficult to get up early to greet at the door Sunday morning or to have to get up early and welcome those coming to the Community Center for food.

However, I want to challenge you not to have the box checked as the reason you serve. Instead remember the words Paul wrote to us when he said, *"You are serving the Lord Christ."* So, the next time you get up early or are asked to stay a little longer than planned, keep these words of Paul near as we continue to serve our Lord together.

REACH DEVOTION 6

02

GATHER

**JAYSON COMBS,
FAMILY PASTOR**

LESSON TWO GATHER

What did Sundays look like for you growing up? Did you attend church once a year, once a month or once in the morning? Did you attend church once before lunch and once that night?

_____

_____

_____

Is attending church a fond memory or a dark memory?

_____

_____

What do Sundays look like for you now?

_____

_____

Acts 2:42-47 describes what "Sundays" looked like in the first century: ***"And they devoted themselves to the apostles' teaching and the fellowship, to the breaking of bread and the prayers. And awe came upon every soul, and many wonders and signs were being done through the apostles. And all who believed were together and had all things in common. And they were selling their possessions and belongings and distributing the proceeds to all, as any had need. And day by day, attending the temple together and breaking bread in their homes, they received their food with glad and generous hearts, praising God and having favor with all the people. And the Lord added to their number day by day those who were being saved."***

After reading Acts 2:42-47, highlight and share what specific *actions* the early church gathered together and did.

_____

_____

_____

LESSON TWO GATHER

Did they only meet on Sunday?

_____

_____

_____

Do any of these *actions* come easy for you? If so which ones?

_____

_____

_____

Are any of these *actions* difficult for you? If so which ones?

_____

_____

_____

On a scale of 1-10 (10 being the highest), how important are these *actions* as you gather with other believers?

_____ Studying Doctrine

_____ Prayer

_____ Fellowship

_____ Offering

_____ Praising God

_____ Unity

_____ Seeing people saved

Colossians 3:15-16 says, *"And let the peace of Christ rule in your hearts, to which indeed you were called in one body. And be thankful. Let the word of Christ dwell in you richly, teaching and admonishing one another in all wisdom, singing psalms and hymns and spiritual songs, with thankfulness in your hearts to God."*

LESSON TWO GATHER

Ephesians 5:19 adds, *"Addressing one another in psalms and hymns and spiritual songs, singing and making melody to the Lord with your heart."*

What do these verses tell us we should be doing as we gather together with other believers?

_____

_____

_____

Tim Keller said, "Every Christian should be able to give both teaching (the ordinary words for instruction) and admonition (a common word for strong, life changing counsel) that convey others the teaching of the Bible."

Do you agree with this quote?

_____

_____

_____

If these actions are what the church is called to do, then why do my Sundays (or other days that I gather with other believers) feel so different? Shamefully, as a Pastor, there are many times I struggle to focus on these things as I gather together with the Church. In my position as a Pastor, I can find myself focusing on so many other distractions. Instead of focusing on what God wants me to focus on during a gathering, I find myself focusing on how loud the music is, when to go up on stage for announcements, or the baby who is sitting in the second row crying their eyes out. All of us, at times, end up in distraction mode when we gather together. However, we must work on focusing on what God has for us.

39

LESSON TWO GATHER

Are there any weekly distractions that are hindering you as you gather together with the church?

_____

_____

_____

If you have children in school, you understand the processing of getting them ready every morning. Sometimes it can be a crazy fight. There is the list of things that must get done before you can walk out the door. The first item on the check list is to wake up everyone. You prepare breakfast. Everyone needs to get dressed. You make sure that every child has brushed their teeth and combed their hair. Lastly, you grab all the stuff needed for school and get out the door in a timely manner. I know in my home, sometimes it is a big struggle to get ready.

The next time you gather I want you to think about this process of getting yourself ready. What things do you need to set down (figuratively) before you come?

_____

_____

_____

What verses can you read to get your heart ready for His Spirit to move?

_____

_____

_____

What should be your prayer before you enter the gathering?

_____

_____

_____

LESSON TWO GATHER

"The basic trouble with the church today is her unworthy concept of God... Our religion is weak because our God is weak... Christianity at any given time is strong or weak depending on her concept of God." A.W. Tozer

LESSON TWO GATHER

NO LONGER SLAVES

GATHER, DEVOTION 1
Isaiah Combs | *Worship Leader & Young Adults Director*

Two years ago, if you would have told me I would be the worship leader at The River Church in Holly, I would have laughed and given you a bunch of excuses as to why I cannot be the worship leader. I would have complained, "I am not skilled enough" or "I do not know music that well." The list of excuses would continue until you gave up on me.

God has a funny way of equipping the called and not calling the equipped (You might want to think about that phrase for a moment).

We think God does not know we are not good enough. We fool ourselves into thinking God does not know that we are not smart enough.

The Bible shows that Moses had this same problem. When God told him to go back to Egypt and that He was going to use Moses to free His people from slavery, Moses panicked and made excuses. God even let him know that when the people are free, Moses was going to be the leader of God's people. Moses' initial reaction was to make excuses, "I do not speak well."

God ends up using Moses in an incredible way and even uses him through what Moses thought were his shortcomings.

We sing a song on the weekends called *"No Longer Slaves"* by Jonathan David and Melissa Helser. It is one of my favorite songs.

GATHER DEVOTION 1

The verses talk about God delivering us from our enemies and how we were chosen in our mother's womb to do incredible things for God. So, there is no reason to fear.

The chorus says, *"I'm no longer a slave to fear, I am a child of God."*

I love singing or saying that I am a child of God. I was bought with a price and freed from my slavery to sin. From now on, I have no reason to fear death, hell, or the grave; no man can stand against me. I do not know about you, but that is incredibly freeing.

However, the best part of the song is the bridge:

"You split the sea so I could walk right through it. My fears were drowned in perfect love. You rescued me so I could stand and sing I am a child of God."

That is so powerful. It is just like when God called Moses and used him even though he thought he was not good enough. God then split the Red Sea so Moses and the Israelites could walk through it.

God wants to split the seas in your life so you can do incredible things for Him. So, you can stand and yell it to the world that you are free from fear, a child of God.

God had a great plan for Moses, He has great plans for me, and He has great plans for you.

IN THE PRESENCE OF JEHOVAH

GATHER, DEVOTION 2
Debbie Kerr | *Office Administrator*

"I will bless the Lord at all times, his praise will continually be in my mouth." Psalm 34:1

It was late December 2007. The world was preparing for the busiest, and some would say, the most wonderful time of the year. While this frenzy of activity was going on in the world, my cousin Bruce and his wife Jennifer sat in a doctor's office in Indianapolis, Indiana. They were a godly couple that loved Jesus and served in the church for many years. They had a strong faith and knew God was good in all things. One day Jennifer noticed a lump on the back of her neck. She went to the doctor, and they ran some tests. Within days the doctor called Bruce and Jennifer back into the office and delivered the most devastating news anyone could hear. It was cancer! There were not a lot of warm fuzzy words about her prognosis, and very little hope was given. While still in the doctor's office, Jennifer looked at Bruce and said seven of the most powerful words that have impacted my faith to this day. She said, "There's no panic in the throne room." Wow! I am not sure I would have that same reaction; I believe I would eventually get there, but it might take me a minute or 500. But here she is only moments after hearing this terrifying news, and she is ministering to her husband assuring him that her faith is still strong. Jennifer lived six more months, just long enough to see her precious daughter graduate from high school.

In June 2008, my parents and I traveled to Indianapolis to attend Jennifer's funeral. The service was so beautiful and God-honoring. It highlighted how Jennifer's life consistently pointed people to Jesus.

It was obvious that she impacted many lives. After the service, the family gathered for a meal in Bruce and Jennifer's beautiful home. I walked around and looked at every picture and every Scripture verse that had been thoughtfully placed on the walls. I could not get enough and wanted to know as much as I could about this amazing woman. As I looked around, I noticed a den off the foyer with a baby grand piano. As you can imagine, I was very curious to see what was most likely the last song played in that room. I respectfully walked in and looked at the sheet music resting there, and I was instantly undone. "In the Presence of Jehovah" was one of my all-time favorite worship songs. Before we headed home that day, Bruce shared with me that during the last few months, he would wake up in the middle of the night to find Jennifer missing from their bed. He would make his way downstairs to find Jennifer sitting at the piano quietly worshipping the God she knew and trusted so well. Bruce said, he would sit on the floor next to her in those darkest moments, as she worshipped. She was not waiting to be transported to her Heavenly home; she was the kind of lady that lived daily in His presence. Jennifer had an intimacy with Jesus that I have rarely seen in all my years as a Christian. It has been nine years since her death, and I have never forgotten the blessing and inspiration I received from her that day. Worship has an amazing way of replacing the focus from ourselves and our circumstances to our faithful and loving Jehovah God.

"In The Presence of Jehovah"

In and out of situations
That tug of war at me;
All day long I struggle
For answers that I need.
But then I come into His presence
And all my questions become clear

And for a sacred moment
No doubt can interfere.

Chorus
In the presence of Jehovah
God Almighty, Prince of Peace,
Troubles vanish, hearts are mended
In the presence of the King.

Through His love the Lord provided
A place for us to rest;
A place to find the answers
In the hours of distress.
Now there is never any reason
For you to give up in despair;
Just slip away and breathe His name
He will surely meet you there.

GATHER DEVOTION 2

LAMB OF GOD

GATHER, DEVOTION 3
Richie Henson | *Production Director*

The most profound truth for all times is that Jesus, the Son of God, came down to be the ultimate sacrifice and payment for our sins. As profound as this truth is, it remains unmistakably simple. This simplicity is eloquently expressed in the song *"Lamb of God."*

The Lamb of God in my place
Your blood poured out my sin erased
It was my death You died I am raised to life
Hallelujah the Lamb of God

Jesus died on our behalf to pay a debt of sin we could never overcome, pulling us out of death and into life. What a beautiful truth that we get to spend everyday living in Heaven.

I believe there are times when we feel our sin is so complicated that salvation must be complicated. We think that there must be some other knowledge or understanding that we need to fully grasp God and our faith in Him. However, we must learn to embrace the beauty of the simplicity.

I think this truth is evidenced by the apostle Paul in 1 Corinthians 2:1-2 (NLT), *"When I first came to you, dear brothers and sisters, I didn't use lofty words and impressive wisdom to tell you God's secret plan. For I decided that while I was with you I would forget everything except Jesus Christ, the one who was crucified."*

GATHER DEVOTION 3

If anyone had the ability and authority to complicate the message of the Gospel, it was Paul. Paul was an Old Testament scholar having all the ability and tact in the world to express the deepest truths of the Word of God. However, Paul felt it necessary to forsake all other messages except Jesus Christ as Messiah.

The Bible is full of rich truths, but only one is necessary for salvation. Jesus died, was buried, and rose again on our behalf. If we could simply cling to the reality of our Savior, I believe we would see this city and state changed for Jesus in a radical way. As we sing Lamb of God, it creates a special moment for all of us to let go of the complexity of life and faith, just spending a moment affirming our faith in the foundational truth of Jesus as Messiah.

REVELATION SONG

GATHER, DEVOTION 4
Sierra Combs | *Women's Ministry Director*

"At once I was in the Spirit, and behold, a throne stood in heaven, with one seated on the throne. And he who sat there had the appearance of jasper and carnelian, and around the throne was a rainbow that had the appearance of an emerald...From the throne came flashes of lightning, and rumblings and peals of thunder, and before the throne were burning seven torches of fire, which are the seven spirits of God, and before the throne there was as it were a sea of glass, like crystal. And around the throne, on each side of the throne, are four living creatures...and day and night they never cease to say, 'Holy, holy, holy, is the Lord God Almighty, who was and is and is to come!'" Revelation 4:2-8

There has never been a time when music was not my thing. I love it. Even when I am not singing, strumming, humming, or listening, I am doing one of those things in my head. It is like I have my personal movie soundtrack going on in my head, and it is pretty awesome. God has gifted me with a musical heart, mind, and ear, and in recent years, He has taken this shy, terrified, quiet girl and given me boldness and passion to help lead His people in worship. It is just my favorite thing. Every Saturday night, I go to bed excited to wake up to gather together to worship our incredible God with my church family. Every Sunday morning, He wakes me up at 5:30 am in a good mood, which is truly miraculous because I am not a morning person and on any other day even having to get up at eight is like pulling teeth. However, that is not the case on Sundays. I love the church and worshiping together is important.

GATHER DEVOTION 4

As a worship leader, there is nothing better for me than seeing and hearing the church put everything aside and focus their hearts on singing praise to God. There are so many songs that hold much meaning to me, but there is one in particular that gets me every time. I often have held back tears of joy when singing or hearing it because I think, this is awesome now but WOW! This is only just a small imperfect preview of my eternal future in Heaven- sitting around the throne room of God with absolutely no other purpose but to worship the King of the Universe. The song, *"Revelation Song,"* is practically plucked straight from Scripture, as you can see from above. Also check out Ezekiel 1:25-28. I love to sing the chorus to this song.

Holy, Holy, Holy, is the Lord God Almighty,
who was and is and is to come.
With all creation, I sing, praise to the King of Kings,
You are my everything, and I will adore You!

I just close my eyes and think about what it will one day be like in Heaven. With all creation, I will sing praises to Him who sits on the throne. I long for that day. I agree as the song continues.

Filled with wonder, awestruck wonder, at the mention of [His] name.
Jesus Your name is power, breath, and living water!
Such a marvelous mystery!

That is so true! The fact that God loves us so much that He left that glorious throne room to come to Earth as a man and pay the penalty for our sins is a straight up marvelous mystery. The awesome thing is that if you have accepted Him as your Lord and Savior, you will be standing beside me one day singing praises to the Lamb that was slain. I pray I see you there. In the meantime, we can and should keep practicing here while we wait!

GREAT ARE YOU, LORD

GATHER, DEVOTION 5
Josh Lahring | *Production Director*

This life is full of hurt, pain, and brokenness. Many times when my heart has been so broken and overwhelmed over the years, all there is to do is sing a song to deal with the hurt. Sometimes there is nothing like singing praise to God in the midst of pain. He is the healer, the restorer, and our hope. In the time of pain, I have proclaimed this truth in song.

"Great Are You Lord" by All the Sons and Daughters.
You give life, You are love, You bring light to the darkness
You give hope, You restore every heart that is broken
It's Your breath in our lungs, so we pour out our praise to You only.
And all the earth will shout Your praise
Our hearts will cry, these bones will sing
Great are You, Lord

In Genesis 2:7 it says, ***"Then the Lord God formed the man of dust from the ground and breathed into his nostrils the breath of life, and the man became a living creature."*** God gave Adam the breath of life, and this was an eternal breath. There was no death and Adam was perfect. Then we sinned and brought death upon ourselves, and that breath was taken away. Death entered the world.

But God restored us. He sent His perfect Son, Jesus as our new eternal breath of life.

GATHER DEVOTION 5

Romans 8:10-11 says, *"But if Christ is in you, although the body is dead because of sin, the Spirit is life because of righteousness. If the Spirit of him who raised Jesus from the dead dwells in you, he who raised Christ Jesus from the dead will also give life to your mortal bodies through his Spirit who dwells in you."*

Jesus is the life of our bodies, and every breath we have belongs to Him. What else can we do with that breath than use it for His glory? We sing praises to His name and not only that, but everywhere we go we proclaim His name and everything we speak should honor Him. On that day when He returns, we will continue with the whole earth in shouting His praise, proclaiming that Jesus is Lord.

O PRAISE THE NAME (ANASTASIAS)

GATHER, DEVOTION 6
John Hubbard | *Worship Leader*

There are so many reasons that a song can make an instant connection to a body of believers. From the very start of the first verse, it can grab your attention and take you to a place of affirmation even as you are listening for the first time. *"O Praise the Name (Anastasis)"* by Hillsong Worship is a song that wastes no time getting to the point, the Gospel. This song is a journey through the death, burial, and resurrection of Jesus. The word "Anastasis" is a Greek word that translates to "resurrection," not only regarding Jesus, but also the raising up of believers at the end of the age.

Not only is *O Praise the Name* a journey, but it is also sung from a personal point of view. The first line, *"I cast my mind to Calvary,"* brings the listener to an actual point of reference. The second line, *"where Jesus bled and died for me,"* hits you with one of the most vivid scenes found in the Gospel. The songwriters wanted to hone in on the actual moment of Jesus' death and step into the shoes of those that were closest to Him. The second verse has a line, *"His body bound and drenched in tears,"* is a unique look at that moment between Jesus' death and resurrection. A lot of the time it seems that the burial of Jesus suffers from the middle-child syndrome, not as in-your-face as the eldest child who came first, Jesus' death, and not like the youngest child who everyone likes to give their attention, His resurrection. To spend a moment and think about the people who lost all hope and had to bury Jesus, you cannot help but feel that raw emotional reaction.

GATHER DEVOTION 6

The chorus is my favorite part of the song, and I love that every arrangement I have heard has at least three in a row to end the song. Most of the time having three in a row makes you feel like it drags on, but the lyrics catch you:

O praise the Name of the Lord our God
O praise His Name forevermore
For endless days we will sing Your praise
Oh Lord oh Lord our God

Forevermore we will sing His praise, so if you are sick of singing that after the third time I do not want to be the one to tell you what we will be doing in Heaven before the throne of God, forever and ever. To be fair, I am sure that eventually, I will want to switch up the song now and then, but until that time comes, I will continue to praise the Name of the Lord our God.

GATHER DEVOTION 6

03

GROW

JOHN CARTER,
DIRECTOR OF OPERATIONS

LESSON THREE GROW

When was the last time you tried to grow something?

_____

_____

_____

Was it easy for you?

_____

_____

_____

Did it happen overnight?

_____

_____

_____

Did the effort produce some significant value for you?

_____

_____

_____

When I consider the previous questions and what is involved in growing; a few words come to mind: commitment, time, effort, and consistency. It really does not matter what the objective is, whether you are trying to grow a garden, run a Spartan Race, hit a certain weight, or obtain a particular position in your career, the following words pretty much describe what it takes: commitment, time, effort, and consistency. The same four words can be used to describe how you can grow spiritually as well.

I believe **commitment** is where it starts. We all have ideas; however, to how many of those ideas are we committed? For example, I really like the idea of having a garden in my backyard. It could be a place where I can go with my kids and pick out fresh vegetables and fruit.

LESSON THREE GROW

I mean, who would not like this idea? If a garden could just be put in the backyard and it grew on its own, life would be perfect. If we did not have to till or weed the ground or water it, I think everyone would have a garden. But everyone does not have a garden for obvious reasons, me included. We have to start with what is our commitment level to the desired objective.

Name something you thought was a good idea, but ended up not being something to which you were super committed.

_____

_____

_____

The first part of Proverbs chapter 16 is a pretty common passage to hear in the church. Verses 1-3 say, *"The plans of the heart belong to man, but the answer of the tongue is from the LORD. All the ways of a man are pure in his own eyes, but the LORD weighs the spirit. Commit your work to the LORD, and your plans will be established."* Notice the word, *"commit."*

How committed are you to your own personal spiritual growth?

_____

_____

_____

How do you take it from a good idea to being something to which you are truly committed?

_____

_____

_____

Time: We all only get 24 hours in a day. It is a difficult thing to manage for sure; this is one of the areas with which I struggle. I wish

LESSON THREE GROW

there were 25 hours in the day so I could get all the things I need to finish. As I mature, I find it more and more difficult to do all the things I want to do. Unfortunately, that means saying "no." If you are like me, that can be difficult. Being committed to growing spiritually means we have to make the time for it. This can look different for everyone so there is not a one-size-fits-all.

I cannot help but be convicted when I read Matthew 5:33-37, *"Again you have heard that it was said to those of old, 'You shall not swear falsely, but shall perform to the Lord what you have sworn.' But I say to you, Do not take an oath at all, either by heaven, for it is the throne of God, or by the earth, for it is his footstool, or by Jerusalem, for it is the city of the great King. And do not take an oath by your head, for you cannot make one hair white or black. Let what you say be simply 'Yes' or 'No'; anything more than this comes from evil."*

Think of a time when you were over committed, what was the first thing that suffered?

_____

_____

_____

Have you ever said, part of the reason I do not read my Bible or pray as often as I should is because I just do not have time?

_____

_____

_____

Making time for your commitment means you might have to prioritize your time, and learn to say "no" to things that are not helping you meet your responsibility. If growing spiritually is a commitment of yours, evaluate how your time is being used, and adjust if you

LESSON THREE GROW

see the need. The one-on-one time with God, the Creator of the Universe, is priceless.

Effort: It is when the good idea gets old. Committing to run a race, making the time to run three times a week is all good. At least until week four hits and your muscles hurt, it is not fun, and the commitment to run a race just does not matter to you anymore. There are many things that individuals can list as being a great idea but a little while into it, the effort just goes away. I think of New Year's resolutions, diet plans, and exercise goals as things that can easily lose their luster after awhile.

What is something you can think of that might fall into this category as effort draining?

_____

_____

_____

One of my all-time favorite passages that help me with effort is Hebrews 12:1-4, *"Therefore, since we are surrounded by so great a cloud of witnesses, let us also lay aside every weight, and sin which clings so closely, and let us run with endurance the race that is set before us, looking to Jesus, the founder and perfecter of our faith, who for the joy that was set before him endured the cross, despising the shame, and is seated at the right hand of the throne of God. Consider him who endured from sinners such hostility against himself, so that you may not grow weary or fainthearted. In your struggle against sin you have not yet resisted to the point of shedding your blood."*

When the going gets tough, this is the passage on which I often focus. Trust me when I say, that as a Christian the going gets tough. Life, Satan, and our stinking flesh will do everything it can to keep

LESSON THREE GROW

us from following through on our commitment to growing closer to God. Just remember what Jesus did for us, a little effort does not even begin to compare to all that Jesus has done for us.

What do you rely on when the "going gets tough?"

_____

_____

_____

Consistency: Probably one of the hardest things in life is to be consistent. Once you can be consistent with your commitment, it changes from being a commitment to becoming part of a lifestyle. Hopefully, the things you are committing to are the things you want to be part of your life. The promise that God gives us in James 4:7-8 is clear, *"Submit yourselves therefore to God. Resist the devil, and he will flee from you. Draw near to God, and he will draw near to you."*

What is one thing where you are really consistent?

_____

_____

_____

What is one thing at which you wish you were really consistent?

_____

_____

_____

If you truly desire to be closer to God, it starts with an individual commitment to draw near to God. It involves making the time, putting in the effort, and then doing those things consistently. I know it is easier said than done! Putting four words on a piece of paper is not that hard, putting those four words into practice is super hard.

LESSON THREE GROW

Take some time and reflect on things that you are truly committed to accomplishing. Have you wanted to be a part of a growth community? Maybe you desire to read more of the Bible? How about praying a little more to God? Maybe you are new to the whole follow "Jesus thing," and do not even know where to start. The promise James gives us is a solid one. My own experience and walk is a testimony that there will be many times when following Jesus is not the most comfortable. God might ask you to do something crazy, like lead a growth community. He might ask you to preach at a nursing home. He may ask you to go to prison. He may ask you to be kind to someone when your natural instinct is not to be nice. It is all part of drawing closer to God.

What is one thing you can commit to doing right now to draw closer to God?

_____

_____

_____

Do not be afraid to share that one thing with someone, it makes it harder to back out.

LESSON THREE GROW

LESSON THREE GROW

MILK, MEAT, AND APPLES

GROW, DEVOTION 1
Donna Fox | *Assistant to the Growth Pastor*

We have some apple trees in our yard. They have been there for quite some time and produced apples in abundance! One of the trees was producing fruit year after year and suddenly died. We had to remove it. The remaining trees continue to produce apples. That one tree produced good fruit until it died.

Some trees live for many years and never produce fruit, or at least good fruit. They do not have good soil or do not receive enough sunlight or water. The life of the tree may be long, but the fruit is not good. People are the same. Some keep growing, maturing, and producing fruit until the day they die. Some just "exist," not maturing or producing fruit.

We continue to grow physically as we age. But more importantly, we must continue to grow in maturity. God has placed us here to be used by Him until the day we leave this Earth. Whether you are 20, 50, or 90 years old, being in the Word, listening to sermons, and praying, we continue to grow in God's Word and share the Good News with others. I have a friend whose mother has Alzheimer's and even though she cannot remember names, or recent events, she sings hymns all day long and is ministering to the staff and visitors at the nursing home. God still uses her for His glory! I had another dear friend who has now passed on to eternal life with her Heavenly Father. In her last years, she could not walk or see, but she could pray. She prayed day and night for our leaders, our country, and individuals. She was one of the godliest women I have ever met and was used by God until the day she died. She never stopped

GROW DEVOTION 1

learning, growing, and maturing in her relationship with her Lord and Savior.

The Bible speaks of producing fruit, vines, and branches over and over. John 15:5 is an example of this, *"I am the vine; you are the branches. Whoever abides in me and I in him, he it is that bears much fruit, for apart from me you can do nothing."* Also, Matthew 7:17 adds, *"So, every healthy tree bears good fruit, but the diseased tree bears bad fruit"* (Hint – the disease is sin.).

Just because we grow old does not mean we are mature, especially spiritually mature. Oswald Chambers said, "Spiritual maturity is not reached by the passing of the years, but by obedience to the will of God."

New Christian's need spiritual milk (1 Corinthians 3:2; 1 Peter 2:2; Hebrews 5:12). But as we learn the Word of God, grow in our relationship with Jesus, listen to the teaching of the Holy Spirit, and follow the will of God (turning away from sin), then we begin to mature spiritually and begin to long for the meat (solid food). 1 Corinthians 3:1-3 says, *"But I, brothers, could not address you as spiritual people, but as people of the flesh, as infants in Christ. I fed you with milk, not solid food, for you were not ready for it. And even now you are not yet ready, for you are still of the flesh."*

Are you ready for the solid food? Or are you content drinking milk? God desires more for you. He wants a relationship with you that is not just superficial; it is meaningful and deep. It is reading the Bible, it is praying, and it is sharing your "story" (testimony) and His "story" (the Gospel) with others. Be like the apple tree and continue to produce fruit until your end on Earth. Do not waste a day!

GROWTH TAKES TIME

GROW, DEVOTION 2
Michael Fox | *Creative Director*

Growth takes time. I was reminded of this recently through my son's school project, and I remember the same project from when I was a child. He brought home a white Styrofoam cup full of soil, with grass seed planted in it. The instructions were to regularly add water and place in the sunlight. After some time, grass would grow. I have always been amazed watching things grow from almost nothing. A little seed can transform into some really neat and different things, but it always takes time.

Recently, I was reflecting on my spiritual growth over time. I know in my life there have been many high times of growth and also many low times of growth. I wondered why we are called to grow. I began to read an article from allaboutgod.com which pointed me to 2 Peter 1:3-8.

2 Peter 1:3-8 says, *"His divine power has granted to us all things that pertain to life and godliness, through the knowledge of him who called us to his own glory and excellence, by which he has granted to us his precious and very great promises, so that through them you may become partakers of the divine nature, having escaped from the corruption that is in the world because of sinful desire. For this very reason, make every effort to supplement your faith with virtue, and virtue with knowledge, and knowledge with self-control, and self-control with steadfastness, and steadfastness with godliness, and godliness with brotherly affection, and brotherly affection with love. For if these qualities are yours and are increasing, they*

GROW DEVOTION 2

keep you from being ineffective or unfruitful in the knowledge of our Lord Jesus Christ."

The article goes on to summarize that spiritual growth is becoming more like Jesus Christ. Paul says in 1 Corinthians 11:1, *"Be imitators of me, as I am of Christ."*

I know that one of my goals in serving Jesus with my life is to share His love for others and what Jesus did for them by dying on the cross and saving them. The best way I know to do this is to imitate Him, and others will see Christ through me. This is a large task, one that I will work towards for the rest of my life. 2 Peter chapter 1 mentions knowledge, self-control, steadfastness, and godliness; these are all qualities I hope to develop in my daily life. We are called to study God's Word to gain knowledge. The passage also states, *"For if these qualities are yours and are increasing, they keep you from being ineffective."* I want to be effective in serving God, and I need knowledge in Him to be effective.

I desire to increase in His knowledge. Practically, for me, this looks like surrounding myself with other believers in a Growth Community, who will help point me towards God's Word and continue growing. Growing takes time.

70

THE PATH TO THE PRIZE

GROW, DEVOTION 3
Holly Boston | *Women's Ministry Director*

"I press on toward the goal for the prize of the upward call of God in Christ Jesus." Philippians 3:14

We spend our lives setting goals to improve or grow. As a student growing up, my goal was straight A's, a 4.0. As an athlete, I tried to score as many goals as possible during my soccer games. In track, my goal was to have the fastest time in the 100-yard dash. It is hard to believe that I, "Smalls," had the high school record for the 100-yard dash. I would tell you my time if I could remember. As an employee, annual reviews assess my success in achieving last year's goals and establish new ones. As a mother of a child with Autism, every year I attend an IEP to help teachers assess his progress and establish achievable goals.

As I prepared for my growth community this fall, I began to think about my goals for the year with the ladies. It occurred to me that we are good at asking for prayer for spouses, children, family, friends, and even situations. But rarely do I see prayer for personal spiritual growth. Do we have spiritual goals? If not, how do we know we are growing in Christ?

On the first night, I told the ladies that my desire for them this year was not merely knowledge of the Bible, but spiritual growth. Most of them looked like deer caught in headlights. Immediately, I saw our need and began to list some practical steps for growth. As with all areas of life, we need to know our long-term goal. Matthew chapter 28 defines our goal as Christians to **"Go, therefore and**

GROW DEVOTION 3

make disciples of all nations..." (verse 19). We are to do this as *"ambassadors of Christ, God making his appeal through us"* (2 Corinthians 5:20). To be effective messengers for Christ, we must hear the Word of God, know the Word of God, and do the Word of God (James 1:22). To that end, I have found five necessary steps to grow in Christ:

Determination: Growth in any area of life begins with determination. There are some commands in God's Word I have found very difficult to swallow. If I had waited until I felt like submitting, humbling myself, forgiving the one who hurt me or loving my enemy, it would never have happened. It always begins with a choice: choosing to obey God regardless of how I feel. Joshua 24:15 says: *"...chose this day whom you will serve..."* The choices are usually Jesus or self.

Devotion: Psalm 37:4 says: *"Delight yourself in the LORD, and he will give you the desires of your heart."* To delight in the Lord means to experience His goodness. This can only occur by spending time in prayer, study, and obedience.

Desire: At first glance, one might think that Psalm 37:4 is saying if we spend time with God, He will give us what we want. It is interesting though, when you spend time with God, in prayer and study, He begins to rearrange your heart. Suddenly, you find your priorities and desires lining up with His. The desire to spend time with God becomes #1 on the "To do list."

Discernment: When Paul prayed for the Christians of Philippi, he prayed for *"...knowledge and discernment..."* so that they would know what is best and right. Paul knew such understanding could only come from Jesus Christ (Philippians 1:9-11). It is the Holy Spirit within that teaches and guides us. Praying before studying the Word or deciding how to respond to situations is crucial.

GROW DEVOTION 3

Display: All the knowledge and understanding in the world is useless if we do not apply it to our lives. We are called to **"put on the new self"** (Colossians 3:10). We are to reflect the light of Christ to draw others to Him. Lord, may they see more of you and less of us.

So, how is your spiritual growth? Are you determined to grow in Christ? Do you devote time to the Lord; cultivating a desire to live for Christ? If you are waiting for life to settle down, for the time to fit it in your schedule, the time will never come. Put Him first, and the rest will fall into place. In the words of Nike: Just Do It!

GROW DEVOTION 3

INTENTIONAL

GROW, DEVOTION 4
Ken Perry

"Growth," think about that word for a moment. What images does it bring up in your mind? If you are like me, pictures of your childhood come flooding into memory. I remember my dad taking the training wheels off of my bike and the exhilaration of finally being able to ride with the big boys. I remember moving from tee ball to swinging at a pitch thrown by an adult. I am brought back to milestone school graduations like fifth grade, eighth grade and what seemed like an eternity for most of us, twelfth grade (Thankfully, the pictures are locked away somewhere).

Each passing year brought that "joy-filled" trip for new school clothes because you just did not fit the old ones anymore. Thankfully, I am built differently than my brother, so hand-me-downs was not an option. I would be willing to bet you that your memories included snapshots of different times in your life also. Day by day and week by week we grew until one day we stopped. Our physical growth process has a natural ending designed in each of us by God as we are fearfully and wonderfully made.

There is, however, another kind of growth that should have no end. In 2 Peter 3:18, the Apostle exhorts the beloved, ***"Grow in the grace and knowledge of our Lord and Savior Jesus Christ. To Him be the glory both now and to the day of eternity. Amen."*** Our spiritual growth as Christians is not a suggestion; it is a necessity. 1 Timothy 4:7 (NLT) says, ***"Do not waste time arguing over godless ideas and old wives' tales. Instead, train yourself to be godly."*** There is discipline involved. It will not happen on its own.

GROW DEVOTION 4

The Apostle Paul wrote this in Philippians 3:12-13 (NLT), *"I don't mean to say that I have already achieved these things or that I have already reached perfection. But I press on to possess that perfection for which Christ Jesus first possessed me. No, dear brothers and sisters, I have not achieved it, but I focus on this one thing: Forgetting the past and looking forward to what lies ahead, I press on to reach the end of the race and receive the heavenly prize for which God, through Christ Jesus, is calling us."* Think about this for a moment. When Paul wrote these words, he is in a Roman prison toward the end of his life. He is a very mature Christian, yet he tells them he has not arrived. We are to grow, we are to train, and we are to press on no matter what stage of life we find ourselves.

If spiritual maturity is the goal of every Christian, then with all humility, we must be teachable people. We must be willing to ask the hard questions that demand honest answers. Am I in the same spot spiritually as I was last year? How have I grown since becoming a believer? If asked, would others say they see growth in me? If the answers are less than you would want, then by all means, decide to become proactive in your growth. Maybe you can join a Growth Community where you are exposed to more mature believers. Perhaps you can download a reading plan that takes you through the Bible in a year. Whatever it is, decide to intentionally pursue knowledge of God and a stronger relationship with Him. It is a lifelong endeavor that bears much fruit. Make spiritual growth a priority in your life and be able to say, like Paul, I have pressed on and attained the Heavenly prize.

SPIRITUAL GROWTH

GROW, DEVOTION 5
Holly Wells | *Assistant to Lead Pastor Jim Combs*

Running a marathon was on my bucket list years ago, and it was completed by the time I was twenty years old. I got "the bug" and went on to run my second, third, fourth, fifth, sixth, and now I think I have done somewhere around ten marathons over the years (I stopped counting). I remember those I have run well and certainly remember those I could have done better. All have been completed. I did most having trained well, maintaining discipline and diet, mostly injury-free, leaving all that I had out on those courses, and while having a good time! Then, there have been those that I was a little too lax in being diligent to put in the work, the time, the effort, the right fuel, and to no surprise, it was a fight to get through those 26.2 miles (and yes, the .2 matters!).

Race days have included a variety of weather, though mostly the dry heat of Southern California, but my favorite was running in a torrential downpour through the flooded streets of Los Angeles to the Santa Monica Pier. I did not set a personal record that day, but man it was fun! I have finished strong with miles that flew by and crossed the finish line "on time" according to how I trained. But there was one race in particular when I realized that how I felt at a mere six miles should have come much later, like at mile markers 20-22. This would be my worse marathon to-date. I fought for every step and battled with my aching, blistered feet, sore knees, and burning hip joints just to keep moving forward. I fought to hold myself up because my back went out in those earlier miles and I tried not to be overtaken by my increasing irritation. I was completely fatigued, but quitting was never an option (and never will be). Although I finished

GROW DEVOTION 5

that day, nothing about it was done well including the days leading up to it. I got out what I put in.

The same applies to our spiritual growth. The depth, the strength, and the maturity reflected in our relationships with God start with us. Someone once told me they were in a backslidden state, and I quickly countered with, "Well, you can front-slide, too!" It is true! We decide if we are moving forward with the Lord, or not. We determine if we are going to or not going to know Him more deeply. We are in control of our dedication to follow, seek, listen, obey, and love Him more. Just as we choose to invest in a new friendship or a relationship and decide how much attention we give our time to learn about that person, the same applies to our pursuit of the Lord. But know this: we are either moving forward or backward with God; we choose. Sure, we can go to church on Sundays, attend a weekly Growth Community, serve in a ministry, event, or gathering, hold a fancy title, and throw out some "Christianese lingo," but it is the position of our heart that God sees which matters the most (1 Samuel 16:7).

What are we pursuing in our quiet time or when no one is looking? (See Matthew 6:21). How are we applying His Word when someone is rude or hurts us, gossips, or passes judgment about us, when someone interrupts and inconveniences our day, or when we are met with a mean-spirited or unforgiving heart (or are we harboring the hardened heart and unforgiveness?)? (See Matthew 7:4-5; 18:21-35; Colossians 3:12-15; 1 Peter 3:8-12). What about giving someone what they do not deserve? (See Jude 1:22-23). Do we have a growing burden for the lost, the broken, and the forgotten, the "less thans?" (See Matthew 25:34-40; James 1:27). Do our words and conduct build others up or tear people down? (See Luke 6:45; Proverbs 13:12; Colossians 3:8-10; Hebrews 10:24-25). Do we seek, experience, and respond to God's conviction in our lives?

GROW DEVOTION 5

(See Romans 3:10; Hebrews 12:5-6; 1 John 1:9). Do we ask Him how to pray, do we pray according to our agendas, or is it some repeated script to simply check off a box? (See Matthew 6:5-13; Philippians 4:6-8; James 5:16; 1 Thessalonians 5:16-18). Do our lives increasingly reflect His working and refining? (See Matthew 7:15-20; Jeremiah 17:7-8; James 3:17-18). Can we see proof that though we are not sinless, we are sinning less? (See Ephesians 4:17-32). You know what it is for you.

The bottom line is we are either going to choose to grow in the world, or we will choose to grow in the Lord. No matter how young or old we are in the Lord, none of us have "arrived." None of us have learned and applied the entire Word of God flawlessly. We all need to seek Him more than we did the day before. We all need to be more intentional rather than on cruise-control. Will we choose to pursue Him more than we pursue the latest fashion, reality T.V. show, the newest video game, relationship, food, hobby, social media, or the time it takes to get ready in the morning? We have no valid excuses. There are tons of resources if you do not know where to start (if you have a Bible, start in the book of John). Holiness does not happen through osmosis; you have to apply yourself. I dare you to invite God into "all" that you do including your quiet time, Bible study, conversations, relationships, driving, fishing, shopping, and running. It is exciting to see what will happen. You have to work; you have to train. What you put into your relationship with God will be reflected by what comes out of it.

"All athletes are disciplined in their training. They do it to win a prize that will fade away, but we do it for an eternal prize. So I run with purpose in every step. I am not just shadowboxing. I discipline my body like an athlete, training it to do what it should. Otherwise, I fear that after preaching to others I myself might be disqualified." 1 Corinthians 9:25-27 (NLT)

GROW DEVOTION 5

STARTING STRONG

GROW, DEVOTION 6
James Mann | *Children's Director*

"*Therefore, as you received Christ Jesus the Lord, so walk in him, rooted and built up in him and established in the faith, just as you were taught, abounding in thanksgiving.*" Colossians 2:6-7

As the Children's Director at our Goodrich location, I am constantly working on building a firm spiritual foundation for our children to ensure their walk with God is the best that it can be. Many people begin their walk with God but never go anywhere with it. They are starting a race, and barely crossing the starting line. God commands us to dive into His Word and pray to Him for understanding. This is a key starting point in our growth. Many people, like myself, struggle with this. We have so much going on in our day to day, that focusing on our growth is pushed to the back burner. We are all guilty of this to some degree.

After finishing my bachelor's degree, I decided it was time to take my spiritual growth seriously. I was noticing that my plateaued growth was no longer just affecting me, but my students as well. I was not setting a good example for them. I decided that I was going to begin my master's degree, in pastoral studies, to get my growth back on track. Now, I am not saying that everyone should go out and get a Bible degree, but this is what made the most sense in my life. Since starting this journey, I have noticed a change in my walk. I am enjoying my time with God, and I am getting more from my studies. Growing with God has become less of a chore and more of an enjoyable thing to do. Like it says in Colossians, if we have truly

GROW DEVOTION 6

received Christ Jesus, then we should be walking in Him and have our roots be established in Him. We are not following God's will for us if we are not taking the time to grow. Sometimes we need to go out of our way and prioritize our time. God desires for us to draw closer to Him through reading His Word and talking with Him. As believers, we should have the same desire.

GROW DEVOTION 6

04

INERRANCY OF SCRIPTURE

DR. RANDY T. JOHNSON, GROWTH PASTOR

LESSON FOUR INERRANCY OF SCRIPTURE

The Bible is the number one best seller of all time. There is nothing like the Bible. It has no equal. It is like no other book in history. Though the world is filled with books, the Bible stands alone. N.T. Wright said, "The Bible is the book of my life. It's the book I live with, the book I live by, the book I want to die by."

What makes the Bible special, unique, and valuable?

_____

_____

_____

Why is the Bible the first topic covered in this series?

_____

_____

_____

Norman Geisler said, "The inerrancy of Scripture is the foundational doctrine in which all other doctrines rest, and the Psalmist rightly said, 'If the foundation be destroyed, then what can the righteous do?'"

God has revealed Himself in three main ways. First, He has revealed Himself through nature (Romans 1:19-20). Second, He revealed Himself through His Son, Jesus (John 14:9). Third, He revealed Himself through His Word, the Bible.

Are there other ways in which you believe God reveals Himself?

_____

_____

_____

It is vital that we understand why we can trust God's Word. It is necessary in order to comprehend all other disciplines. Inspiration,

LESSON FOUR INERRANCY OF SCRIPTURE

infallibility, and inerrancy are all part of understanding the power, particularity, and perfection of God's Word.

1. Inspiration

The Bible is from God (breathed out by God) through human writers. It is not just "inspired" by God, it is directly from Him. He breathed out the words.

2 Timothy 3:16 expresses this truth, *"All Scripture is breathed out by God and profitable for teaching, for reproof, for correction, and for training in righteousness."*

How should the Bible be used?

_____

_____

_____

2 Peter 1:20-21 adds insight into this discipline, *"Knowing this first of all, that no prophecy of Scripture comes from someone's own interpretation. For no prophecy was ever produced by the will of man, but men spoke from God as they were carried along by the Holy Spirit."*

How did the men who wrote the Bible get their words?

_____

_____

_____

1 Thessalonians 2:13 continues this concept, *"And we also thank God constantly for this, that when you received the word of God, which you heard from us, you accepted it not as the word of men but as what it really is, the word of God, which is at work in you believers."*

LESSON FOUR INERRANCY OF SCRIPTURE

Since God cannot lie, what does it say about His Word?

_____

_____

_____

2. Infallibility

The Bible cannot fall or fail. The Bible is clear; God is all-knowing and all-powerful, so His Word will stand.

Matthew 5:18 points out, *"For truly, I say to you, until heaven and earth pass away, not an iota, not a dot, will pass from the Law until all is accomplished."*

According to this verse, how precise is God's Word?

_____

_____

_____

Isaiah 40:8 says, *"The grass withers, the flower fades, but the word of our God will stand forever."*

How can these verses challenge us?

_____

_____

_____

How can these verses comfort us?

_____

_____

_____

LESSON FOUR INERRANCY OF SCRIPTURE

"Even though the Bible is an ancient document, every person in every situation in every society that's ever existed can find in this book things that endure forever. Here's a book that never needs another edition. It never needs to be edited, never has to be updated, is never out of date or obsolete. It speaks to us as pointedly and directly as it ever has to anyone in any century since it was written. It's so pure that it lasts forever." John MacArthur

3. Inerrancy

The Bible is without errors. There are no discrepancies. It never contradicts itself. It not only contains truth, but it is also the truth.

John 17:17 says, *"Sanctify them in the truth; your word is truth."*

If the Bible has errors, does it make God (and Jesus) a liar?

_____

_____

_____

What problems arise if God (and Jesus) is a liar?

_____

_____

_____

"The Bible is the Word of God, and God cannot err. So, to deny inerrancy, rightly understood, is to attack the very character of God. Those who deny inerrancy, soon enter the dangerous terrain of denying all Scriptural authority for both doctrine and practice."
Ravi Zacharias

"To forsake the inerrancy of Scripture is to snuff humanity's only candle of truth. Inerrancy is the ship's rudder, the traveler's compass, the lamp to our feet and light to our path." Ray Comfort

LESSON FOUR INERRANCY OF SCRIPTURE

The Bible gives an accurate account of history, but it also tells the future. One of the strongest points expressing the uniqueness of the Bible is fulfilled prophecy. The Old Testament contains prophecy, and some of it has already been fulfilled.

Here are twelve (of some 330) fulfilled prophecies that help show the truth of God's Word. Note how much earlier the prophecy was written and describe the event.

Genesis 49:8-10 (written about 1,500 years beforehand)
Matthew 1:1-3; Revelation 5:5   _____

Micah 5:2 (written about 700 years beforehand)
Matthew 2:1-6   _____

Isaiah 9:7 (written about 700 years beforehand)
Matthew 1:1   _____

Psalm 72:10-11 (written about 1,000 years beforehand)
Matthew 2:1-11   _____

Jeremiah 31:15 (written about 600 years beforehand)
Matthew 2:16-18   _____

Zechariah 9:9 (written about 500 years beforehand)
Mark 11:1-10   _____

Isaiah 29:18; 35:5 (written about 700 years beforehand)
Matthew 11:5   _____

Exodus 12:46; Psalm 34:20 (written about 1,500 years beforehand)
John 19:31-36   _____

LESSON FOUR INERRANCY OF SCRIPTURE

Micah 5:1 (written about 700 years beforehand)
Matthew 27:30   _____

Psalm 22:16; Zechariah 12:10 (written about 1,000 years beforehand)
John 20:25-29   _____

Psalm 22:18 (written about 1,000 years beforehand)
John 19:23-24   _____

Zechariah 11:12-13 (written about 500 years beforehand)
Matthew 27:5-8   _____

Franklin Graham said, "History and human nature prove the truth of the Bible every day, but the greatest evidence is seen in changed lives that cannot be denied. This infallible Book is its own great commentary: 'The entirety of Your word, Lord, is truth' (Psalm 119:160)."

How should the inerrancy of Scripture affect our lives?

_____

_____

_____

Why does this discipline need to be one of *The Majors*?

_____

_____

_____

"A Bible that's falling apart usually belongs to someone who isn't."
Charles H. Spurgeon

LESSON FOUR INERRANCY OF SCRIPTURE

Duet. 18:15-22
Blc it was writ 1500 years
ago, 40 authors it's
not one historical inaccuracy

LESSON FOUR INERRANCY OF SCRIPTURE

2 TIMOTHY 3:16-17

INERRANCY OF SCRIPTURE, DEVOTION 1
Chuck Lindsey | *Reach Pastor*

"All Scripture is given by inspiration of God, and is profitable for doctrine, for reproof, for correction, for instruction in righteousness, that the man of God may be complete, thoroughly equipped for every good work." 2 Timothy 3:16-17 (NKJV)

Three cheers for any of you who are reading this with an actual Bible sitting next to you. I am not including any of these sissy digital "Bibles" on phones, tablets, and computers! I am talking about one that has pages you have to turn by hand, pages so thin that your highlighter is going to mark some obscure passage on the backside of that page! The thing is a work of art, complete with ribbons, gold edges, and an embossed cross on the cover. It is a real Bible. It is a Bible that requires a commitment to carry it, both for its visibility and its weight! I am talking about a Bible that can be broken in and worn out through continual use. It is a real Bible. It is the kind that smells the way any proper Bible should, like a dead cow! Are any of my people still out there?

I am of course only joking. I sit every morning and read my Bible on my tablet. I take down notes and highlight passages just as I once did with a physical Bible. I search the Bible on my phone and compare passages while on the go from place to place. I use a computer religiously (pun intended) to study for the various sermons I preach each week. I do all that, with my real Bible sitting next to me as I write this. The truth is, the paper, ribbons, embossing, and leather (that glorious leather) do not make the Bible what it is. That

INERRANCY OF SCRIPTURE DEVOTION 1

is just one way of delivering its content. It is the content, the actual words on those pages, whether physical or digital, audio or visual, that is the show stopper.

There is nothing like the Bible. It has no equal. It is like no other book in history. Though the world is filled with books, the Bible stands alone. It stands alone for one primary reason. One thing sets it apart forever. It comes from God Himself. He wrote it. Oh sure, He used people to physically put pen to paper, but God wrote it. Therefore, it is not the disjointed ramblings of 40 different authors through 66 books. It is one unified message written through thousands of years of human history by God Himself through His people. That changes everything.

This truth is undeniably clear in 2 Timothy 3:16 (NKJV) where it says, *"all Scripture is given by inspiration of God"* (NKJV). The content of the Bible is called "Scripture" because it is more than just advice, conjecture, or opinion. It is bedrock truth because it comes from God Himself. The passage goes on to say, *"all scripture is given."* This means that the writers did not sit down to think about what they would like to write or address. They were "given" what was written. It was given by God. They wrote down, what God gave them to write. It goes on and says, *"all Scripture is given by inspiration of God."* The word translated "inspiration" means "to fill, to breathe." It referred to the filling of the sails of a boat or someone simply breathing. The point is clear. God breathed out His Word, the Bible, giving it to those who loved Him and wrote it down for us.

Because the Bible is the "breathing out" of the actual source of all life, truth, and purpose, the Bible is powerful. The rest of verses 16-17 show us this as we read, *"and is profitable for doctrine* (teaching), *for reproof* (error correcting), *for correction* (showing the right way), *for instruction in righteousness* (growth!) *that the*

INERRANCY OF SCRIPTURE DEVOTION 1

man of God may be complete (grown up), ***thoroughly equipped for every good work*** (ready for everything God sends us to do)."

So grab a Bible, dig in, and have the confidence that every word you are reading comes from God Himself!

INERRANCY OF SCRIPTURE DEVOTION 1

2 PETER 1:20-21

INERRANCY OF SCRIPTURE, DEVOTION 2
James Clouse | *Student Pastor*

My family had grown up Catholic. As a boy, I remember telling my mom and my grandparents that I wanted to be a priest in the Catholic Church. They were so proud of me. It is not an unusual thing as we have had many priests and nuns come from our family. I remember growing up being an altar boy in my grandparents' wedding, going through the catechisms and First Communion.

However, when I became saved, or started a true relationship with Jesus Christ, at the age of 12, my family was confused. Growing up we did not read much of our Bible because at the time it was up to the readers at mass or the priests to interpret the Bible for us. We were not encouraged to read the Bible for ourselves or go to God's Scripture for understanding.

In 2 Peter 1:20-21 we see that the audience of Peter may have been getting some interpretations that did not coincide with the Word of God. It says, *"Knowing this first of all, that no prophecy of Scripture comes from someone's own interpretation. For no prophecy was ever produced by the will of man, but men spoke from God as they were carried along by the Holy Spirit."*

Many through the years have tried to discredit much of the Bible and especially the Old Testament. Prophets of the Old Testament had a job to do, and that was to give the Word of the Lord to an intended audience. Whether that audience was Nineveh, Israel, or a surrounding authority, God had a purpose and design for

INERRANCY OF SCRIPTURE DEVOTION 2

His prophecies. Reading Jeremiah and Lamentations can be an incredibly difficult emotional roller coaster as we see the pain and suffering of Jeremiah the prophet as his audience would not listen to him.

We need to understand today that Scripture is inerrant; which is to say that it is without error. God used many men for an incredible and intentional purpose, and that is to record His Word as given by Him. It is important to remember while the Word was given to them to write, it was God-inspired and God-breathed.

It is also given to us for a reason. God has as much of a purpose for us reading His Word as He had a plan for the people of the Old Testament. As the church, we need to realize that we are led by the Holy Spirit in our lives to help understand the Word that God has given to us. Do not always let other people interpret the Bible for you. Lean on the understanding of the Holy Spirit in your daily devotion. Go to the Lord in fervent prayer to understand and live what you are reading.

1 THESSALONIANS 2:13

INERRANCY OF SCRIPTURE, DEVOTION 3
Ryan Story | *Student Pastor*

Back in my B.C. (before Christ) days I was always put off by Christian arrogance, or at least what I perceived to be arrogance. I had a friend in high school who was a believer; I am pretty sure his name was Dan. I remember one day Dan asked me about Jesus and my views on salvation and what not. I do not remember much about the conversation. Clearly, I did not begin following Jesus at that moment, but I remember being so put off by the idea that this guy put so much faith in the Bible. I recall attacking the validity of the Bible, the flaws in the notion that God inspired men to write it, and every other naive argument I could raise. Oddly, one thing I cannot forget about this conversation was my closing remark to him. Not listening or giving him a chance, I remember looking at Dan saying, "You put so much faith in a book as your guide to life, well *"Hop on Pop"* is the book I choose to put my faith in, what is the difference?" For years I thought I was so clever. I know I used this in different arguments with other Christians, but I look at it now and realize how flawed, immature, and unintelligent I was. It is weird that God never lets this conversation be forgotten. Fast forward eight or so years after that conversation and I sit here typing this as a person who went to college and majored in Biblical Studies. As a pastor, I am a person who is figuring out how to most effectively teach Scripture. It has become an all-consuming obsession of mine. God sure is funny sometimes.

Sadly, I have seen Christians live their lives as if *"Hop on Pop"* was at the same level as the Bible. Maybe it is not exactly *"Hop on Pop"* but living as if a book is at the same level as the Bible. Clearly,

INERRANCY OF SCRIPTURE DEVOTION 3

we scoff at the notion of putting a Dr. Seuss classic on the same level as the Bible, but honestly, at times we let other books become more influential in our walk with God. I have fallen victim to reading Christian books by some of my favorite pastors instead of reading the Bible. I love the mindsets of David Platt, Francis Chan, Charles Spurgeon, and Oswald Chambers but reading these books is not the same as reading the Bible. *"Crazy Love"* and *"Radical"* are not cannon. Reading those books is not bad, but I caught myself reading peoples' perspectives of the Bible more than I was reading the Bible itself. We must make sure the one book we saturate our selves in reading comes from a source that is everlasting, powerful, and true.

1 Thessalonians 2:13 says, ***"And we also thank God constantly for this, that when you received the word of God, which you heard from us, you accepted it not as the word of men but as what it really is, the word of God, which is at work in you believers."*** Paul is making a big claim, and as an unbeliever, I could not understand this. Paul is telling people to realize that the things Paul writes about are not just Paul's opinion or Paul's motives. The things Paul wrote about were the Word of God. The reality is the Bible did not just fall from Heaven; God used men to pen it. We live in such a cynical indecisive culture that we pick apart and argue about everything. Since God is real, then God's Word is true. If God's Word is the Bible, then the Bible must true.

After a few years of living for Jesus, I spun my *"Hop on Pop"* argument to help me witness to unsaved high browed individuals, like my former self. The thing that makes the Bible perfect is its author. *"Hop on Pop's"* truth can only go as far as how powerful Dr. Seuss was. Since the Bible's truth comes from its author; therefore, its truth can go on for eternity. Since the Bible's author has the power to lead someone from death to life, I think we can put a high degree of certainty that the Bible is true.

INERRANCY OF SCRIPTURE DEVOTION 3

The idea that Scripture is inspired and infallible is a fundamental cornerstone of living for Jesus. This notion cannot be shifted, moved, or even up for debate. Everything in our lives hinges on if the Bible is true or not. If one part of the Bible is not true, then everything can fall apart behind it. In our lives, if we make one part of the Bible to be opinion or a guideline and not a command, everything in our lives will fall apart behind that notion.

The reason the Bible is true is not based on the men who penned it; it is based on the real God that told them what to write. Since an everlasting, Holy, true, powerful God said something, you can pretty much take that as truth.

INERRANCY OF SCRIPTURE DEVOTION 4

JOHN 17:17

INERRANCY OF SCRIPTURE, DEVOTION 4
Joshua Combs | *Lead Pastor*

"Sanctify them in the truth; your word is truth."** John 17:17

The night that Jesus was betrayed, He prayed for me. He prayed for you. He prayed **"...for those who will believe in me through [the apostles'] word"** (John 17:20). He prayed for unity in the church. He prayed that we would see His glory. He prayed that we would love the Father and each other. He prayed that the heavenly Father would keep us from the evil one. He prayed that God would sanctify us, setting us apart for His holy purpose and service.

Jesus prays, simultaneously teaching us, that the cleansing (sanctification) process would happen through truth. In John 8:32, Jesus is confronting the religious leaders and says, **"...you will know the truth, and the truth will set you free."** The truth is what purifies our hearts and sets us free from the flesh, releasing the powerful clutches of sin that enslaves us. But what is the truth? In Jesus' High-Priestly prayer in John chapter 17, He concretely states, **"...your word is truth."**

Truth is a major theme in the Gospel of John. Only hours after the High Priestly prayer, Jesus tells Pilot, **"...I have come into the world – to bear witness to the truth"** (John 18:37). But what Jesus states is profoundly important. Jesus has both called Himself truth (John 14:6) and referred to God's Word as truth. What Jesus means is crucial for every believer to understand. Jesus declares the unchanging reality that God's Word, the Scripture, is Truth.

INERRANCY OF SCRIPTURE DEVOTION 4

It is through the truth of the Bible that we understand God's infinitely perfect glory, the depth of our sin, and see the redemptive plan of God unfolding and fulfilled in Jesus Christ. The truth not only helps us see the glorious nature and plan of God but truly leads us to love Jesus, the Truth (John 14:6), more. This is so simple and yet so profound. When we read the Scripture, we discover the unchanging truth of God who is Jesus, who sets us free from sin and *"...cleanse us from all unrighteousness."* We must daily commit to being in the Truth (Scripture) so that we may know the Truth (Jesus, our Savior).

ISAIAH 40:8

INERRANCY OF SCRIPTURE, DEVOTION 5
Caleb Combs | *Gathering Pastor*

If you live in Michigan or a place that experiences the four seasons, you probably love fall. Fall is the greatest time to be outside with all of the colors at a cider mill, play sports, or just get out for a walk. The colors are breathtaking, the air is crisp, and the scents are delightful. I love all football, cider, and donuts, but one thing I never look forward to is raking leaves. I have eight mature oak trees on my half acre lot that love to torture me. Hundreds and hundreds of bags later, my yard is clear from leaves, but man is it a ton of work. The life of a leaf is interesting. Its birth in the spring and death in the fall make for a short life. All things go through seasons; things come, and things go. Ecclesiastes 3:1 says, ***"For everything there is a season, and a time for every matter under heaven."*** A band called The Byrds wrote a song in 1965 called "Turn, Turn, Turn" based off of this exact chapter, and it turned out to be hit in the United States and the United Kingdom; it's still played and sung to this day!

The words of this verse say it all, ***"for everything there is a season."*** Isaiah 40:8 tells us, ***"the grass withers, the flower fades, but the word of our God will stand forever."*** Things come and go, fads come in style and leave as quick as they came. My kids loved the fidget spinners for a couple of weeks (weird craze in my opinion), but now those things are just lost among the pile of other old toy fads that came and went. We all can think of something that has come into style and now is not, yet we own it. I still like cargo shorts! Ha Ha! However, the book of Isaiah is clear, though everything may fade away and lose relevance, the Word of the Lord will not ever lose

105

INERRANCY OF SCRIPTURE DEVOTION 5

relevance. God's Word is the same yesterday, today, and forever. When our world seems to be turned upside down by tragedies, God's Word is something we can stand on. God's Word says He will never leave you or forsake you, and that is something that you can take to the bank no matter what the circumstance. So today in the business of your life, know this: when all things come and go, His Word will never leave.

MATTHEW 5:18

INERRANCY OF SCRIPTURE, DEVOTION 6
Jayson Combs | *Family Pastor*

"You get nothing! You lose! Good day sir!" This is the climax of the legendary film, *"Willy Wonka and the Chocolate Factory."* This is where the movie gets serious. Gene Wilder, aka Willy Wonka, exploded on Charlie (the main character) by telling Charlie that he had violated the factory contract. The movie revolved around five children who are specially chosen to take a tour of the mysterious Wonka Chocolate Factory. When the children first entered the chocolate factory, they signed a seemingly unimportant contract. The font size of the letters was very large at the top of the contract, but as the words continued, the font size got smaller and smaller until it was impossible to read. All the children signed anyway. At the end of the movie, Willy Wonka revealed that Charlie did not follow all the rules of the contract. At which point, Willy Wonka had to pull out a magnifying glass to read the fine print of the contract.

In Matthew 5:18 (KJV) Jesus says, **"For verily I say unto you, Till heaven and earth pass, one jot or one tittle shall in no wise pass from the law, till all be fulfilled."** A "jot" is the tenth letter of the Hebrew alphabet and is also the smallest letter. The **"tittle"** is most likely a small dash that is only a part of a letter. Here is an example below.

Jesus says that not even the smallest letter or stroke will pass away from God's word. In fact, Jesus places the Old Testament in the highest regard, signifying that all of the Old Testament, even the

INERRANCY OF SCRIPTURE DEVOTION 6

fine print, is true and completely from God. Later in Matthew, Jesus speaks of words again. But this time, He does not speak of the words of the Old Testament. *"Heaven and earth will pass away, but my words will not pass away"* (Matthew 24:35). He says, *"My words."* Jesus is now speaking of His own words here on earth. With this revelation, Jesus "equates his own words with the word of God," as MacArthur explains, and therefore makes the claim that He is God.

In the 1970's, the makers of *"Star Wars"* searched for a toy company to make action figures for their movie characters. All of the big toy companies turned down the proposals (Obviously, this was before the first movie came out). Finally, they found a small toy company out of Cincinnati called Kenner that received a very favorable contract. As we all know, *"Star Wars"* soon became one of the greatest movie franchises of all time, making Kenner millions of dollars. Contractually, Kenner was required to pay the makers of *"Star Wars"* a mere $10,000 a year to maintain the contract, a small iota of their earnings. As years went by: however, someone forgot to read the fine print and did not send the $10,000 check. The contract became void and cost the toy company millions and millions of dollars to get it back.

The word of the Lord is so important. We are blessed to have it in our homes, on our computers, and on our phones. Do not miss out on all that the Bible offers. I want to challenge you to have it in your heart. It is powerful, and every little detail Jesus says is true. Remember this the next time you decide to skip your Bible time.

INERRANCY OF SCRIPTURE DEVOTION 6

05

SALVATION BY FAITH & GRACE OF GOD

DR. RANDY T. JOHNSON,
GROWTH PASTOR

LESSON FIVE SALVATION BY FAITH & GRACE OF GOD

God created man and woman. He gave them one commandment, and they broke it; they sinned. It broke the relationship between God and us. God promised to send One who would be the bridge. For thousands of years, the people of Israel offered sacrifices striving to repair their connection with God. Finally, Jesus (the Messiah and God's Son) came to earth, lived a perfect life, died on the cross for our sins, was buried, and rose again offering us life. This "salvation" is by His grace and is called a gift.

What are some of the best gifts you have given or received?

_____

_____

_____

Ephesians 2:8-9 is one of the clearest passages on this topic, *"For by grace you have been saved through faith. And this is not your own doing; it is the gift of God, not a result of works, so that no one may boast."*

What are some things people do trying to please God or get saved?

_____

_____

_____

According to this passage, how can one be saved?

_____

_____

_____

"Grace means undeserved kindness. It is the gift of God to man the moment he sees he is unworthy of God's favor." Dwight L. Moody

111

LESSON FIVE SALVATION BY FAITH & GRACE OF GOD

Romans 3:20-24 adds to the conversation, *"For by works of the law no human being will be justified in his sight, since through the law comes knowledge of sin. But now the righteousness of God has been manifested apart from the law, although the Law and the Prophets bear witness to it— the righteousness of God through faith in Jesus Christ for all who believe. For there is no distinction: for all have sinned and fall short of the glory of God, and are justified by his grace as a gift, through the redemption that is in Christ Jesus."* I remember the definition of justification as just-as-if-I-never-sinned.

What is the purpose of the law?

_____

_____

_____

According to this passage, what percentage of people have sinned?

_____

_____

_____

"I'm not perfect. And who knows how many times I've fallen short. We all fall short. That's the amazing thing about the grace of God." Tim Tebow

People have never been able to work their way to Heaven. Salvation has always been by the grace of God through faith.

Romans 4:6-8 says, *"Just as David also speaks of the blessing of the one to whom God counts righteousness apart from works: 'Blessed are those whose lawless deeds are forgiven, and whose sins are covered; blessed is the man against whom the Lord will not count his sin.'"*

LESSON FIVE SALVATION BY FAITH & GRACE OF GOD

Was David saved by works?

_____

_____

_____

James 2:23 adds, *"And the Scripture was fulfilled that says, 'Abraham believed God, and it was counted to him as righteousness'—and he was called a friend of God."*

How was Abraham considered righteous?

_____

_____

_____

What does it mean to be called "a friend of God?"

_____

_____

_____

"Saving faith is an immediate relation to Christ, accepting, receiving, resting upon Him alone, for justification, sanctification, and eternal life by virtue of God's grace." Charles Spurgeon

Salvation is by God's grace and through faith alone. This faith is also described as one who believes Jesus is the Son of God. 1 John 5:5 says, *"Who is it that overcomes the world except the one who believes that Jesus is the Son of God?"*

What does *"overcomes the world"* mean?

_____

_____

_____

LESSON FIVE SALVATION BY FAITH & GRACE OF GOD

1 John 5:11-13 adds, *"And this is the testimony, that God gave us eternal life, and this life is in his Son. Whoever has the Son has life; whoever does not have the Son of God does not have life. I write these things to you who believe in the name of the Son of God, that you may know that you have eternal life."*

Can someone know they are saved?

_____

_____

_____

John 1:12 continues, *"But to all who did receive him, who believed in his name, he gave the right to become children of God."*

What are believers called?

_____

_____

_____

"For God so loved the world, that he gave his only Son, that whoever believes in him should not perish but have eternal life." John 3:16

What are the two final destinations?

_____

_____

_____

What does one need to do to have eternal life?

_____

_____

_____

"What gives me the most hope every day is God's grace; knowing that his grace is going to give me the strength for whatever I face, knowing that nothing is a surprise to God." Rick Warren

JOHN 1:12

SALVATION BY FAITH & GRACE OF GOD, DEVOTION 1
Chuck Lindsey | *Reach Pastor*

"But as many as received Him, to them He gave the right to become children of God, to those who believe in His name." John 1:12 (NKJV)

My sister and brother-in-law are foster care parents. In seven years' time, they have provided a home for and cared for over 30 children. Most of these children come from absolutely devastating situations. Many are born addicted to drugs. Others are the only surviving child in a violent home. They come from physical abuse and neglect to sexual abuse and more. Each story is crushing. It is often painful work. It is thankless work. It is late nights, exhausting, tears, fear, frustration, and it can be overwhelming. It is especially painful when that child you love and have cared for, is put back into unacceptable situations. Some have a chance, and some will not make it. It is more than just "hard." With each phone call that comes to take another child, my brother-in-law and sister ask Jesus what He wants them to do. Very often, they say, "Yes, we will take them." We watch them make those children their own until their season together is done. It is thankless work. It is Jesus' work.

Now imagine if the richest man in history began to be burdened for abused children and decided to start doing foster care. Not just foster care, but his goal was the adoption of as many needy kids as possible. What if the richest man in the world began to adopt every child who wanted him? His mission was to make them his children. They would live in his home with him. They would eat from his table. They would bear his name. Each child would, from one day to the

SALVATION BY FAITH & GRACE OF GOD DEVOTION 1

next, move from the devastation they had only ever known to the immeasurable blessing they would now only ever know. All that he has was now theirs. They were his children.

This is what the Bible says has happened to us. It is what God has done for us. From one moment to the next, everything is different. We were lost in our sin and guilt, wandering around in the darkness, without hope, without purpose, and without joy. We were broken people. We were blind people, staggering around in a broken world. We were trying to find anything that seemed like life, anything that resembled purpose, anything that would make us happy even temporarily, and life failed. In every real way, life would fail. The key is "But God." But God stepped into our lives. God stepped in with a mission, a goal, a plan, and a desire to adopt as many as were willing. He went to each lost, broken, and hurting child and offered them life. Therefore, *"as many as received Him, to them He gave the right to become children of God."* We became His own. We bear His name; we are Christians. We will eat at His table and live in His home with Him forever, and all that He has is ours. For, we are His.

And this all happened because we *"received Him"* when He came to us inviting us. We believed in His ability to do what He offered to do. Rejoice you *"children of God"* for He has received you!

1 JOHN 5:5

SALVATION BY FAITH & GRACE OF GOD, DEVOTION 2
Ryan Story | *Student Pastor*

We live in a world with numerous amounts of religions, cults, and philosophies that claim to be able to get people to Heaven, or at least what they claim Heaven to be. Several times a year, I will have a Fusion student ask me, "How do you know faith in Jesus is the only way get to Heaven?" At times, I like to switch up the roles and ask them, "How do you know that Jesus is not the only way to Heaven?" It is enjoyable to watch people come up with a response. However, I feel at these times we can almost take that question as a threat, but as time has passed, I have come to realize that question has more of a longing for comfort in the face of uncertainty. No one in this world likes to walk around with uncertainty especially when it comes to our eternal destination. There are many on both sides of what they have concluded about Jesus. On one side of the coin, the question of "how do you know faith in Jesus is the only way to Heaven" has created a joyful eagerness to see Jesus when our time is up on this Earth. Because of the reassurance and hope putting our faith in Jesus brings, we know the answer to that question. Sadly, on the other side of that coin, we have a large amount of the world that claims that Jesus followers are arrogant, delusional, weak-minded, or flat out wrong.

In 1 John 5:5, it says, ***"Who is it that overcomes the world except the one who believes that Jesus is the Son of God?"*** The world does not want to accept Jesus. In more than just a conflicting ideological way, the world is trying to destroy all things of God. Jesus even says that "if the world hates you remember it first hated me." With all the negativity that the world throws at Christ-followers,

SALVATION BY FAITH & GRACE OF GOD DEVOTION 2

it is easy to forget this amazing verse. This is a simple verse to understand and a powerful verse to memorize and apply. How do we overcome the world? We overcome when we believe in Jesus and what Jesus did for us.

Now back to that amazing question I get asked. I like to respond to that question with "the reason I believe Jesus is the only way to Heaven is I follow the One who has already won." After I get a look of confusion, I elaborate. The reason why Jesus is the only way for us to be saved can be simply put. The only one who can save us from death, Hell, and the grave is to follow the one who was victorious against death, Hell, and the grave. If you follow a person who loses, your outcome will be the same. If you follow someone who is victorious, then you will be victorious. Who is the most victorious person to ever live? If you said Jesus was the answer, then you are correct. The only way for us to be overcomers is simply stated in 1 John, *"believe that Jesus is the Son of God."* All the theological rhetoric that you may or may not fully grasp becomes clear when we simply put our faith in Jesus.

120

ROMANS 3:20-24

SALVATION BY FAITH & GRACE OF GOD, DEVOTION 3
Joshua Combs | Lead Pastor

"*For by works of the law no human being will be justified in His sight...*" Romans 3:20

One of the important truths of the Scripture that we must understand is there has only ever been and only ever will be one means of salvation. For some this may be a radical thought that differs substantially from what you have been taught. Nonetheless, it is true. Throughout the whole of human history, one method of salvation has been given.

Some have, in error, taught that obedience to the Law of Moses was how the saints of the Old Testament were saved and reached the glory of Heaven. Romans 3:20, clearly teaches, "*...by works of the law no human being will be justified....*" Clearly, Abraham, Moses, David, and every other ancient saint was not justified, redeemed, or saved because of their adherence to the Mosaic Law. This principle continues today; no person regardless of the depth of their personal devotion can restore a right relationship with the God of the universe simply by following the letter of the law. Just a few verses later, Paul writes, "*...for all have sinned and fall short of the glory of God.*" We are unable to obey the law (James 2:10). So, if the law does not provide a means of salvation, what is the law's purpose? God has given us the law because "*...through the law comes knowledge of sin*" (3:20). God's Law was given to Moses on Mount Sinai with the sole purpose of revealing how far from God's holiness and perfection we truly are.

SALVATION BY FAITH & GRACE OF GOD DEVOTION 3

That understanding leads us to the great and rather depressing reality that we cannot save or rescue ourselves from God's wrath that is on us. The principle question of this portion of Romans chapter 3 is, "How can we be made right before God?" The Scripture says, *"...the righteousness of God has been manifested apart from the law...the righteousness of God through faith in Jesus Christ for all who believe."*

God in His marvelous grace, sent Jesus to pay the price for our sin on the cross of Calvary. He was buried but rose again on the third day. It is through Christ's atoning work on the cross that the gift of salvation is offered to mankind. We receive that gift, *"...through faith...."* We believe in what Jesus did as the only means to rescue us from the deserved punishment from God that we were facing.

Back to the original point, God's Word gives only one way of restoring a right standing before a Holy God, *"...by grace you have been saved through faith."* Abraham, Moses, David, and the saints prior to the cross looked forward in faith (see Hebrews chapter 11) to the cross, while we look back in faith to the work of Christ on the cross. Salvation has always ever been and always ever will be by grace through faith.

JOHN 3:16

SALVATION BY FAITH & GRACE OF GOD, DEVOTION 4
Tommy Youngquist | *Children's Pastor*

This is most famous verse in all of the Bible! This is the verse that everyone knows, even if they are not religious at all. It is John 3:16!

"For God so loved the world, that he gave his only Son, that whoever believes in him should not perish but have eternal life."

You probably know it by heart. What does it mean? Have you ever stopped to truly digest the words and the meaning behind the message? Here is a quick breakdown.

"For God so loved the world" - There is a God. This God loves us. Humans are God's most precious creation. God's most precious creation made a mistake and sinned. Because of this sin, God's most precious creation was separated from Him. Imagine this scenario. Imagine loving someone so deeply, but you cannot interact with that someone because they made a mistake. God is too holy to interact with the sin that infests humanity. So, God devised a way to get us back to Him and allow us to interact once again.

"That he gave his only Son" - The only way God could reunite His most precious creation to Himself was to sacrifice His Son. He was the only person that could be holy enough to atone for the sins of the world. Do you think God wanted to do this? Would you want to sacrifice your child for someone else? Let me answer that for you... NO WAY! That is how much God's love for us was and is. Despite not wanting to, He did it anyway.

SALVATION BY FAITH & GRACE OF GOD DEVOTION 4

"That whoever believes in him should not perish but have eternal life" - Now what do we do because Jesus, God's Son, paid the ultimate sacrifice? We do like Romans 10:9-10 says, *"Confess with our mouths that Jesus is Lord and believe with our hearts God raised him from the dead."* When we do this, God's Word says that WE WILL BE SAVED! That is how God's love for the world should impact us. It should cause us to believe in Him with everything. It should cause us to love Him in return. It should cause us to want to serve Him with our lives.

As a church, we believe this to be the only way you can attain eternal life in Heaven. Humanity cannot merit salvation in any way. It is simply a belief each person has to make for themselves. Salvation comes by faith in God alone. This is the Gospel. It is the only way God could get us back to Himself. The decision is now up to you. What have you decided? Or what will you decide?

1 JOHN 5:11-13

SALVATION BY FAITH & GRACE OF GOD, DEVOTION 5
Caleb Combs | *Gathering Pastor*

A few years ago, I stopped by my bank on the way home from work to make a deposit. I cannot remember exactly what for, but I am not a huge fan of going to the bank. However, I now love all of the mobile banking apps out there. Sorry, you are not reading to hear about my banking preferences. So, as I walk out of the bank, I hear this lady yelling at me attempting to get my attention. For some reason, I was off of my game that day, I pride myself in being a pretty street smart person, and for some reason, I walked up to a stranger's car in a bank parking lot; yes, not the smartest move I have ever made. As I approached her car, she did something I would never have expected; she began spraying me with cologne. I noticed she had hundreds of bottles in her car and it felt like her goal was to spray me with every one of them! I was caught off guard and was ready to walk away until she said the magic word, well at least the words that caught my attention, "I am running a DEAL today!" This was like magic to my ears; I love a good deal. She said that the bottles normally sell for $75, but today she was selling them for $20. I thought to myself, "How can I pass up on such a good deal?" So, we narrowed down to the best smelling one, and I handed over $20 to a lady in a bank parking lot, and she handed me the merchandise.

Now, I live about 5 minutes from my bank, and so I thought I would surprise my wife with my new smell. I knew she would be so excited about how good of a deal I got and also that I had some semblance of thought on personal smell. So, I sprayed myself a good dozen times on the ride home to the point my car, myself, and probably

SALVATION BY FAITH & GRACE OF GOD DEVOTION 5

those cars around me could recognize how good I smelt! I arrived home and walked in with my chest held high in an attempt to impress my wife. She just looked at me in confusion and asked what I was doing. I moved closer sticking my chest out further hoping she would ask about my smell, and to my amazement, she never did. At this point I was frustrated, so I skipped her asking me and told her the story of my amazing deal and how I thought she would be so impressed with me, but to my dismay, she was not. She just looked at me with a crooked face dissecting what I had just done. She said to me, "I think I recognize that bottle." I responded, "Of course you do, you have seen it at one of your fancy stores!" But she said, "No" and then a light went on, "I know where I have seen that bottle. You can buy it at the dollar store!" At that moment, I realized I had been taken in a bad deal. I was taken for $19 when I thought I had gained so much.

This is an embarrassing story, but one that shows how a bad deal can work. However, Jesus Christ has offered us the best deal of all, the grace of God. Salvation comes by grace and grace alone. It is not something we can earn by doing good things or deserve by living a "good" life. Simply putting our faith in Jesus Christ and trusting in His perfect plan, we too can have eternal life. He does not ask much of us because He already has done the heavy lifting on the cross. He conquered death, Hell, and the grave; His grace covers all of our sins.

We are told a powerful promise in 1 John 5:11-13, *"And this is the testimony, that God gave us eternal life, and this life is in his Son. Whoever has the Son has life; whoever does not have the Son of God does not have life. I write these things to you who believe in the name of the Son of God, that you may know that you have eternal life."* Grace is a free gift; it is the best deal we could ever take. If you have never received this gift, make today the

SALVATION BY FAITH & GRACE OF GOD DEVOTION 5

day. If you have the best deal of all time, make sure you appreciate the work done by Jesus and realize His grace is enough to cover all of your sins: past, present, and future.

SALVATION BY FAITH & GRACE OF GOD DEVOTION 5

EPHESIANS 2:8-10

SALVATION BY FAITH & GRACE OF GOD, DEVOTION 6
Jayson Combs | *Family Pastor*

"For by grace you have been saved through faith. And this is not your own doing; it is the gift of God, not a result of works, so that no one may boast. For we are his workmanship, created in Christ Jesus for good works, which God prepared beforehand, that we should walk in them." Ephesians 2:8-10

Firmly, Awana stands. I grew up as a "church kid." Every Wednesday night, I was a part of a program called Awana, which is a program focused on Scripture memorization. Currently, we have this program at all of our locations. Ephesians 2:8-10 is one of the passages I memorized in Awana that I have never forgotten. I am guilty; however, of skipping right over these verses because I have heard it so many times. We are never done learning, though, and fortunately, I continue to glean truth from passages I have heard over and over. We could spend hours on this particular passage, but I want to focus on four key words for this study.

The first word is *"grace."* Yes, you have probably heard the definition of grace as "unmerited favor," but what does that mean? Paul effectively explains the word grace in Ephesians 2:5. He says that *"even when we were dead in our trespasses, [God] made us alive together with Christ—by grace you have been saved."* In other words, when you had nothing, He gave everything. Romans 5:8 states, *"but God shows his love for us in that while we were still sinners, Christ died for us."* To sin means to reject His ways, and to reject Him. I believe this verse should pull at all believers.

129

SALVATION BY FAITH & GRACE OF GOD DEVOTION 6

Jesus died on the cross even when we were the ones spitting in his face. That, my friends, is grace.

The second word is *"faith."* Yes, it is by grace that we are saved, but Paul also makes a reference to faith in verse 8 (KJV), *"for by grace are ye saved through faith."* Faith is our response to salvation and our action. In chapter 1 verse 13, it says we hear the word of truth, and then we believe. Faith is also a gift of God, like grace (verse 8). It's all His gift to us; grace, faith, and salvation. Therefore, we cannot boast of faith because it is only through God's grace that we have faith. Tony Merida, in Christ Centered Exposition, says, "Faith is the instrument by which we lay hold of Christ."

The third word is *"boast."* When we "get grace," we can understand that boasting about our part in salvation and faith is laughable. Paul says it well in the first chapter of his first letter to Corinthians when he says, *"So that no human being might boast in the presence of God. And because of him you are in Christ Jesus, who became to us wisdom from God, righteousness and sanctification and redemption, so that, as it is written, 'Let the one who boasts, boast in the Lord'"* (1 Corinthians 1:29-31). Church, let us boast in the Lord. Let us boast about Him at our work, with our family, and in our neighborhood.

The final word is *"works."* Scripture clearly says we are not saved because of good works, but rather as followers of Christ, we are created to do good works. Ephesians 4:24 puts it this way, *"put on the new self, created after the likeness of God in true righteousness and holiness."* Again, we do not do good works to be saved, but I believe the reverse is the truth we need to understand. If good works are not evident in our lives and we have no desire to follow Him and to live for him, then where is the salvation? Salvation takes us to good works.

SALVATION BY FAITH & GRACE OF GOD DEVOTION 6

What an amazing passage! I challenge you to memorize this passage and make it part of your life.

06

TRINITY

DR. RANDY T. JOHNSON,
GROWTH PASTOR

LESSON SIX TRINITY

The Godhead eternally exists in three persons: The Father, the Son, and the Holy Spirit. These three are one God, having precisely the same nature, attributes, and perfections. God the Father is fully God. God the Son is fully God. God the Holy Spirit is fully God. The Bible presents this as fact. It does not explain it.

Who are the three persons of the Trinity?

_____
_____
_____

Which one do you relate to most or best? Why?

_____
_____
_____

Four words into the Bible *("In the beginning God")*, we already have the Trinity implied. The Hebrew word used for *"God"* (Elohim) is in the plural form which seems to refer to a triune God. God (Father, Son, and Holy Spirit) created the heavens and the earth.

"All sorts of people are fond of repeating the Christian statement that 'God is love.' But they seem not to notice that the words 'God is love' have no real meaning unless God contains at least two persons. Love is something that one person has for another person. If God was a single person, then before the world was made, He was not love." C.S. Lewis

Explain either point in your own words.

_____
_____
_____

133

LESSON SIX TRINITY

Liberty University declares, "We affirm our belief in one God, infinite Spirit, creator, and sustainer of all things, who exists eternally in three persons, God the Father, God the Son, and God the Holy Spirit. These three are one in essence but distinct in person and function.

We affirm that the Father is the first person of the Trinity and the source of all that God is and does. From Him, the Son is eternally generated, and from Them, the Spirit eternally proceeds. He is the designer of creation, the speaker of revelation, the author of redemption, and the sovereign of history.

We affirm that the Lord Jesus Christ is the second person of the Trinity, eternally begotten from the Father. He is God. He was conceived by the virgin Mary through a miracle of the Holy Spirit. He lives forever as perfect God and perfect man: two distinct natures inseparably united in one person.

We affirm that the Holy Spirit is the third person of the Trinity, proceeding from the Father and the Son and equal in deity. He is the giver of all life, active in the creating and ordering of the universe; He is the agent of inspiration and the new birth; He restrains sin and Satan; and He indwells and sanctifies all believers."

What are the responsibilities of God the Father?

_____

_____

_____

What are the responsibilities of God the Son?

_____

_____

_____

LESSON SIX TRINITY

What are the responsibilities of God the Holy Spirit?

_____

_____

_____

Matthew 28:18-19 says, *"And Jesus came and said to them, 'All authority in heaven and on earth has been given to me. Go therefore and make disciples of all nations, baptizing them in the name of the Father and of the Son and of the Holy Spirit.'"*

What is implied by having all three Persons of the Godhead listed?

_____

_____

_____

Christianity is a monotheistic religion. Mark 12:29 says, *"Jesus answered, 'The most important is, 'Hear, O Israel: The Lord our God, the Lord is one.'"*

How does this verse add to the discussion of a triune God?

_____

_____

_____

"It is commonly said that the Trinity is a mystery. And it certainly is. But it is not a mystery veiled in darkness in which we can only grope and guess. It is a mystery in which we are given to understand that we will never know all there is of God. It is not a mystery that keeps us in the dark, but a mystery in which we are taken by the hand and gradually led into the light." Eugene Peterson

John 1:1 says, *"In the beginning was the Word, and the Word was with God, and the Word was God."* Verse 14 adds, *"And the*

135

LESSON SIX TRINITY

Word became flesh and dwelt among us, and we have seen his glory, glory as of the only Son from the Father, full of grace and truth."

Who was (and is) the Word?

_____

_____

_____

Does this relate to the topic? Why or why not?

_____

_____

_____

Matthew 3:16-17 describes events that happened at the baptism of Jesus, *"And when Jesus was baptized, immediately he went up from the water, and behold, the heavens were opened to him, and he saw the Spirit of God descending like a dove and coming to rest on him; and behold, a voice from heaven said, 'This is my beloved Son, with whom I am well pleased.'"*

How were all three Persons present and involved at the baptism of Jesus?

_____

_____

_____

Acts chapter 5 describes the story of Ananias selling a property and telling the apostles that he gave them all the money. Verses 3-4 record, *"But Peter said, 'Ananias, why has Satan filled your heart to lie to the Holy Spirit and to keep back for yourself part of the proceeds of the land? While it remained unsold, did it not remain your own? And after it was sold, was it not at your*

LESSON SIX TRINITY

disposal? Why is it that you have contrived this deed in your heart? You have not lied to man but to God.'"

Other than the apostles, who did Ananias lie to (two answers)?

_____

_____

_____

2 Corinthians 13:14 adds, *"The grace of the Lord Jesus Christ and the love of God and the fellowship of the Holy Spirit be with you all."*

How does this verse add to the discussion of a triune God?

_____

_____

_____

Why are the different traits (grace, love, and fellowship) associated with each Person?

_____

_____

_____

The belief in the Trinity is essential, but that does not mean we have to fully understand it. John Wesley said, "Bring me a worm that can comprehend a man, and then I will show you a man that can comprehend the Triune God."

LESSON SIX TRINITY

MATTHEW 3:16-17

TRINITY, DEVOTION 1
Ryan Story | *Student Pastor*

I am new to the parent game. Figuring out holiday traditions has been one of the more enjoyable conversations I get to have with my wife. Last Easter, my wife and I decided that we would get our boys gifts that would have to fit into three categories. These categories were, "something fun," "something to wear," and "something to read." We both agreed that we wanted to make sure any books we purchased had some "Jesus merit" to them. While wandering around a Christian bookstore, my wife found cute books about the ark, Bible sight words, and other colorful age-appropriate books for my, at the time, infant son and year-and-a-half son. What did I find you ask? I somehow found a children's book about one of the hardest topics to explain. Yes, I found a children's book that helps explain the Holy Trinity! My wife thought I was insane for getting this book because our sons would not be able to understand the complexity of the Trinity. However, in due time, I know I will need to teach my sons one of the most complex and necessary theological concepts.

The very difficult part of understanding the Trinity is there are only a handful of moments when God is fully present in all three persons. One of the easiest moments to see the Father, the Son, and the Holy Spirit present is when Jesus is baptized. Matthew 3:16-17 says, ***"And when Jesus was baptized, immediately he went up from the water, and behold, the heavens were opened to him, and he saw the Spirit of God descending like a dove and coming to rest on him; and behold, a voice from heaven said, 'This is my beloved Son, with whom I am well pleased.'"*** At this moment we

TRINITY DEVOTION 1

see Jesus, the Son, being baptized. We read the God, the Father, saying that Jesus was "my Son, with whom I am well pleased." Lastly, we see the Spirit of God descending like a dove. The account in Matthew might be the easiest story to see Father, Son, and Spirit all interacting with each other.

We have to understand that God operates in three persons, Father, Son, and Spirit. We also must look at God as one, Father, Son and Spirit are God. We must also know that each person of the Trinity has a different role. All three are all God, but all three "operate" differently. Run that through a few mental filters and when your brain starts to hurt you will be where you need to be when it comes to understanding the Trinity! Many people brush aside complex theology and leave it to a Pastor or scholars, but understanding the Trinity is so important!

When you look at any relationship you have, there are different complexities to it. I am a son of my father and a father to my son. I never treat my son as my father, and my father never treats my son like his son. It is important to understand that how we operate about others brings closeness. Way back in my young adult days I was given the opportunity to preach. At that time, I lived in complex theology, and I wrote a sermon titled *"A Shallow view of the Trinitarian Godhead, Creates a Shallow Doxological Response."* I look back on that and realize I was a bit of a showoff. I should have simply titled this message *"Not Knowing all Three Members of the Trinity Personally, can Affect the Way You Worship God."* This is why Matthew chapter 3 is so important. It is a perfect story to see all three members of the Trinity at work at the same time. At some point, I will have to teach my sons about God as Trinity, and this will be a tough task. I am welcoming the struggle because knowing them all personally will help the way my boys worship.

COLOSSIANS 2:9

TRINITY, DEVOTION 2
James Clouse | *Student Pastor*

As humans, we deal with so many things. Those things are often weird such as puberty and squeaky voices. Sometimes those things tell our age such as grey hairs or wrinkles. Sometimes our bodies do not quite do what we need them to do.

At summer camp with the students, my head and my heart kept telling me that I could do everything they could do. I was running up and down the soccer field, diving for the ball while playing volleyball, or jumping as far as I can in the air to catch a Frisbee in Ultimate Frisbee. While I kept thinking that I could do all this, my body started reminding me that I cannot quite do what I used to do. I was shortly reminded that our bodies experience pain.

This small amount of pain is incomparable to what God the Son did for us. Jesus Christ, as part of the Trinitarian Godhead, came down from Heaven to experience an insurmountable amount of pain. The physical pain and suffering that He experienced cannot even begin to compare with the pain and suffering He felt by being separated from His Father while on the cross.

We can sometimes place so much of an emphasis on Jesus' earthly ministry and forget that Jesus has always been right beside His Father. We always hear about His ministry here but forget that He has always been here and involved with His Father.

Colossians 2:9 says, *"For in him the whole fullness of deity dwells bodily."*

TRINITY DEVOTION 2

When Jesus dwelt here on Earth, He had left Heaven to become God on Earth. We see in John 1:1 that *"In the beginning was the Word, and the Word was with God."* In verse 14 we see that *"the Word became flesh and dwelt among us."* Jesus is the Word that is referenced here. He was there at the beginning of creation, and we read that He will be there at the end during the final days.

The abundance of the Word's love shows in the fact that while Jesus is God, He came down to Earth to experience everything that we experience and more. Having a relationship with Jesus should be easier in knowing that He experienced temptation just as we do. Knowing that Jesus, in His fullness of deity, lived as we do, should make us want to run to Him for comfort and strength.

MATTHEW 28:19

TRINITY, DEVOTION 3
Joshua Combs | *Lead Pastor*

"...the name of the Father and of the Son and of the Holy Spirit...." Matthew 28:19

At the time of Jesus, polytheism (the belief and worship of more than one god or goddess) was the major religious viewpoint. Except for the Jewish Nation, who were monotheistic (believed and worshipped one God), the belief in many gods and goddesses was essentially a globally accepted idea. The prophets of the Old Testament stood against Israel's acceptance of other gods (Deuteronomy 6:4 says, *"Hear, O Israel: The Lord our God, the Lord is one."*), while the apostles in the New Testament spoke against the predominantly Greco-Roman worship of many gods and goddesses. Jesus came and unequivocally declared Himself as God (more about that next week), but made it clear that He was doing only the will of His Father. Other than the cross of Calvary, no greater and more emotional example of this exists than in the Garden of Gethsemane. Jesus prayed, *"My father, if it be possible, let this cup pass from me; nevertheless, not as I will, but as you will"* (Matthew 26:39). Jesus had authority over sickness, disease, demons, weather, and the whole of creation, yet He willingly submitted His will to God the Father. In the same way, Jesus sent the Holy Spirit, the Comforter, telling the disciples, *"He will glorify me, for He will take what is mine and declare it to you"* (John 16:14). We see very plainly in Scripture God the Father, God the Son, and God the Holy Spirit. Please understand, not three gods, but one God in three persons. We would say, the triune God. Christians are not polytheists; we are monotheists. We believe in

TRINITY DEVOTION 3

one God, who exists in three distinct persons. The study of the Trinity is like exploring a profound mystery, and yet within the pages of the Scripture the Father, the Son, and Holy Spirit are seen and more importantly, presented as one.

In Matthew chapter 28 as Jesus is preparing His disciples for His eventual ascension into Heaven, the Lord gives to His followers what we have come to know as "The Great Commission." Jesus charges His followers with the mission of preaching the Gospel throughout the world, and then ***"...baptizing them in the name of the Father and of the Son and of the Holy Spirit...."*** (verse19). The commission to those believers and to us is not to casually be acquainted with or even benign to the Trinitarian existence of God, but to take practical action that acknowledges the Father, Son, and Holy Spirit. Baptism is not necessary for salvation, but a truly saved person will be baptized, publically declaring their faith that God sent His Son to die on the cross and rise again three days later. Jesus then sent the Holy Spirit to guide and comfort us. Even as Jesus, who was baptized by John in Matthew chapter 3, comes up out of the water, the audible voice of God the Father is heard, and the Holy Spirit is seen descending like a dove on Jesus. The Trinity was present at the baptism of Jesus and is present at all future baptisms as well.

2 CORINTHIANS 13:14

TRINITY, DEVOTION 4
Caleb Combs | *Gathering Pastor*

Describing the Trinity is an extremely difficult, if not impossible, task. The word "Trinity" cannot even be found in the Bible, yet it is a crucial piece of our walk and understanding of God. We see the Trinity made up of God the Father, God the Son (Jesus), and God the Holy Spirit. As a child, we sang a song that described the Trinity and its components. The song closed with "three in one, three in one." As a child, and even now, the concept of "three in one" is mind-blowing! I have always said that if someone claims to fully be able to explain the Trinity, then run because they have no idea what they are saying. I am not sure if that is a good statement, but fully understanding the Trinity means to fully understand God and His character and this is something our finite brains can never fully grasp.

Deuteronomy 29:29 says, *"The secret things belong to the Lord our God, but the things that are revealed belong to us and to our children forever, that we may do all the words of this law."* This verse is something that I think every believer must understand. "I realize I cannot fully understand God, yet my faith in Him is willing to trust Him and His plan and my response is to live for Him every day." The Bible tells us that we must have a "child-like" faith to believe in God and this is something that we as followers of Christ must cling to especially when walking through tough concepts like the Trinity.

However, as we look at the Trinity, we see three components that make it up: the Father, the Son, and the Holy Spirit working in unison to establish a relationship with you. 2 Corinthians 13:14 says, *"The*

TRINITY DEVOTION 4

grace of the Lord Jesus Christ and the love of God and the fellowship of the Holy Spirit be with you all." We see the three characteristics of the Trinity described by Paul in 2 Corinthians as grace, love, and fellowship. All three pointing back to the Gospel and God's desire for us to be saved. J. I. Packer, a world renowned theologian, describes the Trinity like this, "The Trinity is the basis of the Gospel, and the Gospel is a declaration of the Trinity in action." The Trinity is three forms of God in action to declare the Gospel to a broken world. The grace of Jesus came to the earth to die on a cross for our sins. The love of God is perfect and true and will never stop pursuing a relationship with us. Finally, the fellowship of the Holy Spirit walks with us everyday, comforting, leading, guiding, and directing our steps. We see all three forms with different characteristics, yet acting in unison pointing us toward a relationship with God. So, just as Paul wrote to the church in Corinth, I write to you, *"May the grace of Jesus Christ, the perfect love of God the Father and fellowship of the Holy Spirit be with you!"* (2 Corinthians 13-14).

MATTHEW 1:23

TRINITY, DEVOTION 5
Chuck Lindsey | *Reach Pastor*

"*Behold, the virgin shall be with child, and bear a Son, and they shall call His name Immanuel, which is translated, 'God with us.'*" Matthew 1:23 (NKJV)

An egg. An apple. Water. What do they have in common? They have all been used to try to explain the doctrine of the Trinity to children and adults alike. The basic concept of the Trinity seems simple on its surface. It is easy to say that God is "three persons in one." But when your five-year-old begins to ask questions, you quickly realize the answer is not so simple. Enter the humble egg as an attempted illustration of the Trinity. It is three parts: shell, white, and yolk existing as one egg. A single apple consists of three parts as well: the skin, the flesh, and the core. Water can exist in three forms, a liquid, a solid (ice), and a gas (steam). These illustrations, however helpful they might be, do not perfectly convey the Trinity (because each "thing" is a different "thing"). Like an exercise bicycle, it feels that the harder you push to understand or explain the Trinity, the more difficult it becomes. However, just because the concept of the Trinity is difficult to wrap our minds around, does not mean that we should disregard it. It is vital!

First things first, the word "Trinity" (a tri-unity - three in one) is not in the Bible. However, the concept is. The Trinity, meaning that the one true God exists in three persons, is taught throughout the Scriptures. We see the doctrine of the Trinity taught from Genesis to Revelation. To understand it, we have to keep it simple. The Bible says that there is ONE God. Deuteronomy 6:4 says, "*Hear O Israel:*

TRINITY DEVOTION 5

The LORD our God, the LORD is one!" We find that not only is the Father called God, but the Son, Jesus is called God, and the Holy Spirit is called God. God is "one."

Jesus is a good starting point. Key passages make it clear that Jesus is God. John 1:1-2 says, *"In the beginning was the Word and the word was with God and was GOD. He was in the beginning with God."* Then verse 14 (NKJV) adds, *"And the Word became flesh and dwelt among us, and we beheld His glory, the glory as of the only begotten of the Father, full of grace and truth."* John 10:30 (NKJV) says, *"I and the Father are One."* Thomas' confession of Him when he saw the risen Jesus is very pointed, *"My Lord and my God!"* (John 20:28 NKJV). Titus 2:13 (NKJV) says that we as His people are *"looking for the blessed hope and glorious appearing of our great God and Savior Jesus Christ."* Colossians 1:15-17 (NKJV) also shows that Jesus is God, *"He is the image of the invisible God, the firstborn over all creation. For by Him all things were created that are in heaven and that are on earth, visible and invisible, whether thrones or dominions or principalities or powers. All things were created through Him and for Him. And He is before all things, and in Him all things consist."* There are many other passages stating Jesus is God. Jesus is called God throughout the Bible.

The Holy Spirit is also God. In Acts chapter 5, we read that Ananias and his wife Sapphira are said to have lied to the Holy Spirit. However, verse 4 (NKJV) says, *"You have not lied to men but to God."* John 6:63 tells us that it is the Holy Spirit who *"gives life."* That is something that only God is said to be able to do. In the Genesis account of Creation, we see the Holy Spirit hovering above the deep (waters) involved in the creation, something that only God is said to have done. The Spirit is said to be all-knowing, everywhere at once, all-powerful, and eternal. These are attributes that only God possesses.

148

On a technical note, in the opening words of the Bible found in Genesis 1:1, we read, *"In the beginning God."* What you may not know is that in Hebrew (the original language of the Old Testament), the word *"God"* there is the plural form of a singular noun. It is "Gods as one" if you will. Not just "gods" making God "polytheistic" (multiple gods), it is describing right from the opening words a "plurality within the one God." Just a few chapters later in the Genesis account, we read of God making man using the words, *"Let us make man in our image."* It is incredible.

The New Testament shows us the Trinity continually. 1 John 5:7 (NKJV) says it clearly, *"For there are three that bear witness in heaven: the Father, the Word, and the Holy Spirit and these three are one."* All three persons of the Trinity are seen together in the Great Commission found in Matthew 28:19 (NKJV), *"Go therefore and make disciples of all the nations, baptizing them in the name of the Father and of the Son and of the Holy Spirit."* At the baptism of Jesus, we see all three persons of the Trinity at once: *"When He had been baptized, Jesus came up immediately from the water; and behold, the heavens were opened to Him, and He saw the Spirit of God descending like a dove and alighting upon Him. And suddenly a voice came from heaven, saying, 'This is My beloved Son, in whom I am well pleased.'"* In Revelation 4:8, we see the angels of God crying out the threefold, *"Holy, Holy, Holy, Lord God Almighty."* They use the word "holy" three times for just one God.

We may not be able to explain how three persons can exist as one God, but that is what the Bible teaches. Perhaps, rather than the picture of an apple or an egg, maybe we should use math? God is not $1+1+1=3$, but rather $1 \times 1 \times 1 = 1$.

TRINITY DEVOTION 5

JOHN 1:1

TRINITY, DEVOTION 6
Jayson Combs | *Family Pastor*

Recently, I visited the Nation of Israel. We went to the Western Wall and watched as many Jews came to the wall to pray to God. The Jews believe this is the closest that they can get to God's glory. The Bible tells us in Exodus 40:34, *"Then the cloud covered the tent of meeting, and the glory of the Lord filled the tabernacle."* We know that the glory of the Lord fell upon the tabernacle. To this day, Jews will go to the Western Wall because this is closest they can get to what is left of the old temple. The sad part is that they have missed where the glory of God is and has gone. The glory of God came as flesh as John chapter one would go on to describe as Jesus.

John 1:1 says, *"In the beginning was the Word, and the Word was with God, and the Word was God."* This verse is so simple that a child could understand it, but yet so deep we could spend months studying it. This chapter is the proclamation that God's glory rests on His Son and that God came down in the flesh as Jesus. Three clear points are made here in verse one. First, the Word was in the beginning. This does not mean a specific period of time. The beginning could also be translated the source. This is saying that the Word was the start. The Word was before all and the source of all. John MacArthur, a biblical teacher and pastor, says, "The word of the Lord was the expression of divining power and wisdom." The second part of this verse says, *"the Word was with God."* This has stated the separation of the Word and God. MacArthur also goes on to say that this is a picture of, "2 personal beings facing one another and enjoying intelligent discourse."

TRINITY DEVOTION 6

Lastly, we have the statement, *"the Word was God."* If you have ever had a Jehovah's Witness come to your door, this is one of the first places they will start. They are okay with the word being the beginning, and the word being with God, but they object to the truth that the *"Word was God."* When we read John 1:14, we see who *"the Word"* is: *"And the Word became flesh and dwelt among us, and we have seen his glory, glory as of the only Son from the Father, full of grace and truth."* The Word (Jesus) became flesh. Jesus took up residence among us.

The wonderful thing about the Bible is that it continually supports itself.

John 1:18 says, *"No one has ever seen God; the only God, who is at the Father's side, he has made him known."*

Colossians 2:9 continues, *"For in him the whole fullness of deity dwells bodily."*

Romans 9:5 adds, *"To them belong the patriarchs, and from their race, according to the flesh, is the Christ, who is God over all, blessed forever. Amen."*

2 Peter 1:1 says, *"To those who have obtained a faith of equal standing with ours by the righteousness of our God and Savior Jesus Christ."*

These verses amazingly describe the Father and Son aspect of the Trinity. I challenge you to read 2 Corinthians chapter 3 to see how the Holy Spirit fits into and completes this Holy Trinity that we trust.

TRINITY DEVOTION 6

07

JESUS IS GOD

DR. RANDY T. JOHNSON,
GROWTH PASTOR

LESSON SEVEN *JESUS IS GOD*

"You say to-MAY-to, I say to-MAH-to." The tomato has taken much scrutiny. Not only is there discrepancy on how to pronounce the word, but there is also debate on whether it is a fruit or vegetable.

Tomatoes are the state vegetable of New Jersey, but they are the official state fruit of Ohio. However, Arkansas resolved the issue by having the tomato be both the state vegetable and the state fruit.

You might be asking, "What is the big deal?" In 1887, U.S. tariff laws imposed a duty on vegetables, but not on fruits. The Supreme Court ruled that tomatoes were to be considered vegetables because they were eaten with the meal and not dessert. However, the courts did not reclassify the tomato botanically; it is still a fruit.

Do you view the tomato as a fruit or vegetable?

_____

_____

_____

Tomatoes are not that big of a deal, but who Jesus is, deserves serious consideration. Was He a good man, a crazy man, or God?

When you picture Jesus in your mind, do you view Him as a man or God? *Both*

_____

_____

_____

The Bible is very clear that Jesus was both a man and God. He was (and is) not "a" God, but God Himself.

155

LESSON SEVEN   JESUS IS GOD

Isaiah 7:14 says, **"Therefore the Lord himself will give you a sign. Behold, the virgin shall conceive and bear a son, and shall call his name Immanuel."** God said that the Messiah would be born even though His mother had never "been with a man." This miracle would be a clear indicator that His Son had arrived. He even tells us His name. **"Immanuel"** means "God with us." When Jesus was born, <u>it meant God was with us because He is God.</u>

What thoughts come to mind when you think of the name Immanuel (or Emmanuel)?

_____
_____
_____

"Emmanuel. God with us. He who resided in Heaven, co-equal and co-eternal with the Father and the Spirit, willingly descended into our world. He breathed our air, felt our pain, knew our sorrows, and died for our sins. He didn't come to frighten us, but to show us the way to warmth and safety." Chuck Swindoll

Isaiah 9:6 adds, **"For to us a child is born, to us a son is given; and the government shall be upon his shoulder, and his name shall be called Wonderful Counselor, Mighty God, Everlasting Father, Prince of Peace."**

Who is the **"child"** this verse is addressing? Does this verse say or imply that the **"son"** is God?

_____
_____
_____

John 1:1 says, **"In the beginning was the Word, and the Word was with God, and the Word was God."** Verse 14 completes a

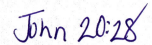
John 20:28

LESSON SEVEN JESUS IS GOD

thought, *"And the Word (Jesus) became flesh and dwelt among us, and we have seen his glory, glory as of the only Son from the Father, full of grace and truth."*

Who is the *"Word?"* What does it say about Him?

The "Word" is Jesus

Even Jesus' enemies knew how He viewed Himself. John 5:18 says, ~5:26 *"This was why the Jews were seeking all the more to kill him, because not only was he breaking the Sabbath, but he was even calling God his own Father, making himself equal with God."*

How did Jesus view and speak of Himself?

he said My Father is working & I am working.

In John 8:58, Jesus makes a very bold statement, *"Jesus said to them, 'Truly, truly, I say to you, before Abraham was, I am.'"* ~came into existence Abraham was about 2,000 years before Jesus. The claim referred back to Exodus 3:14, *"God said to Moses, 'I am who I am.' And he said, 'Say this to the people of Israel: 'I am has sent me to you.'"* God had called Himself *"I Am."* When Jesus called Himself *"I Am,"* He was saying He is God.

What is stated by the tense (past, present, future, or other) of "I Am?"

157

LESSON SEVEN JESUS IS GOD

"A man who was merely a man and said the sort of things Jesus said would not be a great moral teacher. He would either be a lunatic – on a level with the man who says he is a poached egg – or else he would be the Devil of Hell. You must make your choice. Either this man was, and is, the Son of God; or else a madman or something worse. You can shut Him up for a fool, you can spit at Him and kill Him as a demon; or you can fall at His feet and call Him Lord and God. But let us not come with any patronizing nonsense about His being a great human teacher. He has not left that open to us. He did not intend to." C.S. Lewis

In John 10:30-33 Jesus boldly says, *"'I and the Father are one.' The Jews picked up stones again to stone him. Jesus answered them, 'I have shown you many good works from the Father; for which of them are you going to stone me?' The Jews answered him, 'It is not for a good work that we are going to stone you but for blasphemy, because you, being a man, make yourself God.'"*

Which points stand out in this passages?

_____

_____

_____

John 20:28 is short but powerful, *"Thomas answered him, 'My Lord and my God!'"*

What distinction is being made between Lord and God?

_____

_____

_____

"Fundamentally, our Lord's message was Himself. He did not come merely to preach a Gospel; He himself is that Gospel. He did not

LESSON SEVEN JESUS IS GOD

come merely to give bread; He said, 'I am the bread.' He did not come merely to shed light; He said, 'I am the light.' He did not come merely to show the door; He said, 'I am the door.' He did not come merely to name a shepherd; He said, 'I am the shepherd.' He did not come merely to point the way; He said, 'I am the way, the truth, and the life.'" J. Sidlow Baxter

In Colossians 2:9, Paul described Jesus as being God, *"For in him the whole fullness of deity dwells bodily."*

What does this mean?

_____

_____

_____

Paul adds in Philippians 2:5-8, *"Have this mind among yourselves, which is yours in Christ Jesus, who, though he was in the form of God, did not count equality with God a thing to be grasped,* = held *but emptied himself, by taking the form of a servant, being* onto *born in the likeness of men. And being found in human form, he* So he *humbled himself by becoming obedient to the point of death,* put *even death on a cross."* on human form.

What statements express Jesus' deity?

_____

_____

_____

Hebrews 1:1–3 also says, *"Long ago, at many times and in many ways, God spoke to our fathers by the prophets, but in these last days he has spoken to us by his Son, whom he appointed the heir of all things, through whom also he created the world. He is the radiance of the glory of God and the exact imprint*

LESSON SEVEN JESUS IS GOD

of his nature, and he upholds the universe by the word of his power. After making purification for sins, he sat down at the right hand of the Majesty on high."

What statements express Jesus' deity?

_____

_____

_____

"The bodily resurrection of Jesus Christ from the dead is the crowning proof of Christianity. If the resurrection did not take place, then Christianity is a false religion. If it did take place, then Christ is God and the Christian faith is absolute truth." Henry Morris

Matthew 22:
how is it in scripture that
David calls him Lord?

LESSON SEVEN JESUS IS GOD

LESSON SEVEN JESUS IS GOD

JOHN 1:1

JESUS IS GOD, DEVOTION 1
Ryan Story | *Student Pastor*

I enjoy writing devotions. I enjoy getting different topics to study and then write about that topic. I enjoy studying, learning, and writing. This is one of those devotions I did not enjoy writing as much as devotions past. Not because of the topic, the topic of Jesus is God is amazing! Ideas, stories, analogies, and truths that can be applied that flow from this fact are numerous and beyond count! The reason this devotion was not that enjoyable was that in just three words one could sum up every clever, insightful thing I could possibly say: Jesus is God. There is nothing else that needs to be said. Jesus being God is such a fundamental fact in my mind, my mind would not let me go any further. I almost wanted to just increase the size of the font and say, "Jesus is God." Those three words would cover the whole page, and it would be my entire devotion. That is all that needs to be said about this topic.

In the first chapter of the Gospel of John, he starts his account of Jesus' life with some poetry. I love reading the Gospel of John because Matthew, Mark, and Luke write similar styles and even use each other as sources in their accounts. Then you have John who is super poetic and full of imagery. In John 1:1, he says *"In the beginning was the Word, and the Word was with God, and the Word was God."* In John 1:14 he continues, *"And the Word became flesh and dwelt among us, and we have seen his glory, glory as of the only Son from the Father, full of grace and truth."* So we can use some simple deductive reasoning. By looking logically at the premises, we can draw a conclusion. Since *"the Word was God"* that means that God is the Word. Since the *"Word became*

JESUS IS GOD DEVOTION 1

flesh and dwelt among us" means that God became flesh and dwelt among us. Finally, since Jesus was the part of the Trinity that became flesh to dwell among us, that concludes that Jesus is God.

We have already discussed the fact that everything in the Bible is true and comes from the creator of the universe. We must make the fact that "Jesus is God" a truer statement of our lives than us telling ourselves the sun will come up the next morning. "Jesus is God" must be the truest fact in all of our lives.

EXODUS 3:14 & JOHN 8:58

JESUS IS GOD, DEVOTION 2
Joshua Combs | *Lead Pastor*

After shepherding for forty years in absolute obscurity in the Arabian wilderness, God appeared and spoke to Moses. Forty years earlier, Moses had fled Egypt as a murderer and fugitive from Egyptian justice. He now stood with a bush burning before Him, ablaze with the holy glory of God. In this literal Holy Ground moment, God reveals to Moses that He, the Lord, is going to finally free His people from Egyptian bondage and bring them to the long Promised Land. God invites Moses to be His voice to the Pharaoh and the entire nation of Israel. We know from the book of Acts, that Moses while growing up and living like a prince of Egypt, *"...was mighty in his words and deeds"* (Acts 7:22). But that was four decades ago and in Moses' mind, must have felt like a distant dream. Yet, here was God, calling this fugitive shepherd to return to the place of his upbringing and crime, to, through the mighty power of God, deliver the people of God from slavery. Moses trembled before the glory of God and God's call, and asked, *"If I come to the people of Israel and say to them, 'The God of your fathers has sent me to you,' and they ask me, 'What is his name?' what shall I say to them?" And God answered him, 'I AM WHO I AM...Say this to the people of Israel: 'I AM has sent me to you'"* (Exodus 3:13-14). And what followed this conversation was truly one of the most extraordinary sequences of events the world has ever experienced.

Centuries later, Jesus was approached by the Pharisees while He was teaching in the temple. With a great amount of bitterness and venom, they hurled insults at Jesus, even questioning the moral

JESUS IS GOD DEVOTION 2

standing and legitimacy of His birth. As the vicious attacks built to a crescendo, Jesus speaks of Abraham. The Jewish leaders were particularly protective (and possessive) of Abraham, Moses, and King David. Jesus tells them, *"Abraham rejoiced that he would see my day...He saw it and was glad."* Puzzled, the Jewish leaders responded, *"You are not yet fifty years old, and have you seen Abraham?"* Here's the final exchange: *"Jesus said to them, "Truly, truly, I say to you, before Abraham was, I am. So they picked up stones to throw at him, but Jesus hid himself and went out of the temple"* (Acts 8:56-59).

Jesus definitively at this moment declares that He is God, referring back to Exodus chapter 3 and claiming for Himself the name of God. Jesus leaves no doubt for His listeners by saying, *"I AM."* They knew precisely what Jesus was saying. This is proven by the fact that they were so enraged by what they viewed as a blasphemous claim that they instantly went from seething anger to a willingness to commit murder.

This event, among many others in the ministry of Christ, proves that Jesus did not simply claim to be a man deeply in tune with spiritual things, a prophet, or a moral teacher. He claimed to be the God of the Old Testament, the burning bush come in the flesh. At the risk of overstating the point, this is a major of the highest order. Followers of Jesus can never back down from this doctrine which Christ taught. Jesus Christ is God. He was not part of a group of gods nor did He become a God because of His extraordinary life. He was God, is God, and will return one day to earth to visibly demonstrate His authority as God.

166

PHILIPPIANS 2:5-8

JESUS IS GOD, DEVOTION 3
Chuck Lindsey | *Reach Pastor*

"Let this mind be in you which was also in Christ Jesus, who, being in the form of God, did not consider it robbery to be equal with God, but made Himself of no reputation, taking the form of a bondservant, and coming in the likeness of men. And being found in appearance as a man, He humbled Himself and became obedient to the point of death, even the death of the cross." Philippians 2:5-8 (NKJV)

If you asked 100 people to tell you "who Jesus is" you might get 100 different answers! But I tend to believe that those 100 answers would fall into just four basic categories. It is just four separate "buckets" if you will. The first bucket would hold every answer that suggested that Jesus was (as the saying goes) a "good teacher." In other words, He was a religious man, perhaps more religious than others, who taught us about God and His ways. The second bucket would hold every answer given that suggested that Jesus was crazy. Every answer in this bucket would be some form of the idea that Jesus was a lunatic. The thought here is that Jesus was nothing special, but that He (and others) thought He was more than others are. The third bucket would contain all the answers that suggested that Jesus was a fake. These answers would all convey the idea that Jesus knew He was nothing, but pretended to be something to deceive people and lead them astray. The fourth bucket would hold every answer that said that Jesus was indeed who He claimed to be. Jesus was God. He, as God, came to live among us. Every word that came from Him was God speaking. Every work done by Him was God's work. He truly is the Way, the Truth, and the Life as He said.

JESUS IS GOD DEVOTION 3

C.S. Lewis once wrote regarding the answers people might give to the question "who is Jesus:"

"I am trying here to prevent anyone saying the really foolish thing that people often say about Him: I'm ready to accept Jesus as a great moral teacher, but I don't accept his claim to be God. That is the one thing we must not say. A man who was merely a man and said the sort of things Jesus said would not be a great moral teacher. He would either be a lunatic — on the level with the man who says he is a poached egg — or else he would be the Devil of Hell. You must make your choice. Either this man was, and is, the Son of God, or else a madman or something worse. You can shut him up for a fool, you can spit at him and kill him as a demon or you can fall at his feet and call him Lord and God, but let us not come with any patronizing nonsense about his being a great human teacher. He has not left that open to us. He did not intend to. ... Now it seems to me obvious that He was neither a lunatic nor a fiend: and consequently, however strange or terrifying or unlikely it may seem, I have to accept the view that He was and is God."

Jesus is God. He is not "a god" among other "gods." He is not a "lesser god." He is not a "god-like" man who taught us about the true God. There is only one God, and He is that God. He is God, who created all things and brought them into their existence. He is God, and as such, rules over all things and has given you and I life. There was never a moment when He came to be. He has always been. Everything came to be by Him and through His power. He was not created. He created all things.

So, what exactly happened 2,000 years ago? God came down. God came as a baby born to a woman. His name was called Immanuel because it was God now dwelling among us. That baby grew up and eventually took all of our sins upon Himself and died in our place on

JESUS IS GOD DEVOTION 3

a cross. God died for us, for our sin. God came, God died, and then God rose from the dead. Jesus is God.

JESUS IS GOD DEVOTION 3

JOHN 10:30-33

JESUS IS GOD, DEVOTION 4
Caleb Combs | *Gathering Pastor*

"I and the Father are one. The Jews picked up stones again to stone him. Jesus answered them, 'I have shown you many good works from the Father; for which of them are you going to stone me?' The Jews answered him, 'It is not for a good work that we are going to stone you but for blasphemy, because you, being a man, make yourself God.'"
John 10:30-33

"The Son of God became a man to enable men to become sons of God." C.S. Lewis

Jesus said, *"I and the Father are one."* This statement was mind-blowing for the culture Jesus lived in and for our culture today. How could a man actually be God? The crowd responded to Jesus' claim in outrage and were ready to kill Him for this claim. How could this Jesus be a man whose heart beat, perspired when hot, cried when sad, and bled and bruised just like me? This concept is crazy, yet is crucial to understanding our walk with God. You see, Jesus came as a man to experience life as we know it. He was tempted, He grew physically and mentally, and experienced many things a boy and man would experience in that culture, but why? Why would the God of all of the universe come in the form of a man? The answer is simple; it is for you and me!

When Jesus was under trial in front of Pilate and the High Priest, the Pharisees were pushing Pilate to sentence Jesus to death; Pilate was disturbed. He could not find fault with this man, but

JESUS IS GOD DEVOTION 4

they wanted Him killed for one reason, He claimed to be God. This claim brought huge weight and attention from all over Jerusalem and something the religious world did not like. Pilate brought Jesus inside, away from the crowd, to have a conversation with Him. Pilate asked Jesus in John 18:37, *"Then Pilate said to him, 'So you are a king?' Jesus answered, 'You say that I am a king. For this purpose I was born and for this purpose I have come into the world—to bear witness to the truth. Everyone who is of the truth listens to my voice.'"* Jesus came into the world as a reigning King and was born in a barn around animals. There was no pomp and circumstance to His birth, yet the Almighty God was born that day simply on a mission of truth, and that truth would set the captives free!

God stepped out of Heaven and into our earth in the form of a man. This takes faith to believe, but understanding why He did it is crucial to our walk with Christ. He did not do it to waste His time because He was bored in Heaven or that He could come down and punish this world because we had fallen so far away from how He created us. He did it so that He could spread the truth of how much He (God) loves us and desires a relationship with us. Luke 19:10 says, *"For the Son of Man came to seek and to save the lost!"*

ISAIAH 9:6

JESUS IS GOD, DEVOTION 5
Tommy Youngquist | *Children's Pastor*

"The people who walked in darkness have seen a great light; those who dwelt in a land of deep darkness, on them has light shone. You have multiplied the nation; you have increased its joy; they rejoice before you as with joy at the harvest, as they are glad when they divide the spoil. For the yoke of his burden, and the staff for his shoulder, the rod of his oppressor, you have broken as on the day of Midian. For every boot of the tramping warrior in battle tumult and every garment rolled in blood will be burned as fuel for the fire." Isaiah 9:2-5

Holy Smokes! That is some victories right there! Why are all those victories happening to people that are so oppressed? Why are people who have lived in darkness being shone a great light? Why has the rod of oppression been broken? It helps to look at the next verse for the answer.

"For to us a child is born, to us a son is given; and the government shall be upon his shoulder, and his name shall be called Wonderful Counselor, Mighty God, Everlasting Father, Prince of Peace." Isaiah 9:6

Why are all those victories going to happen? The victories will come because Jesus is coming! God is going to make everything right by sending his Son to earth. The Wonderful Counselor is going to reunite God's people with Himself. The Mighty God is going to right all of the wrong in the world. The Everlasting Father is going to take

JESUS IS GOD DEVOTION 5

His children home forever. The Prince of Peace is going to calm the chaos. We have hope!

When I read these verses, I can relate to the person Isaiah mentions in the first five verses. My life seems so oppressed sometimes. It can be oppressed by finances, culture, social, and economic issues and to be frank, people's negativity. I have to remind myself that there is hope. Hope because Jesus is God and Jesus can right the ship. Today, bank on the fact that with Jesus, you get all those victories. Be faithful to Him until you get the win!

JOHN 20:28

JESUS IS GOD, DEVOTION 6
Jayson Combs | *Family Pastor*

Have you ever been mistaken for someone? Has someone ever had a conversation with you and the entire time they thought you were someone else? Sadly, this happens to me all too often in my life. My brother is Pastor Jim, and he is 21 years older than me. This brings great confusion to people when they see me and then, they see him. I cannot tell you how many times people have come to me asking how my father is doing, and then I inform them that I am not who they think I am (I always wonder what people think when they receive my brother's Christmas card with all his children, but I am not in the picture).

In John chapter 20, Jesus has risen from the grave; He has made appearances to many people including some of the disciples. Thomas is one of the disciples who has great doubt that Jesus has risen from the grave because he has yet to see Him. He tells the other disciples that he will only believe if he can see Jesus and can see the scars from the crucifixion. Well, Jesus shows up and Thomas makes this amazing statement in verse 28, *"Thomas answered him, 'My Lord and My God!'"*

Thomas' statement begs the questions, Is Jesus God or did Thomas mistake him for the wrong person? I believe Jesus' response confirms clearly that Jesus is God. If Jesus was not God, do you think He would let Thomas mistakenly call Him King of kings and Lord of lords? As we keep reading the passage, Jesus asks Thomas in the next verse, *"Have you believed because you have seen me?"* If Jesus is not God, I do not believe He would allow Thomas

JESUS IS GOD DEVOTION 6

to call Him God. It would be a very blasphemous statement against God.

Throughout the Bible, there is this beautiful picture of Jesus and God being separate, and being the same. For a fun little study read Daniel 7:9-10 and Revelation 1:12-16. Daniel is clearly referring to God while Revelation is clearly referring to Jesus. Compare the similarities between the two. You will be amazed at how the same characteristics that are used to describe God are the same characteristics to describe Christ Jesus.

JESUS IS GOD DEVOTION 6

08

JESUS WAS SINLESS

DR. RANDY T. JOHNSON, GROWTH PASTOR

LESSON EIGHT JESUS WAS SINLESS

This lesson addresses Jesus as sinless but also includes His virgin birth. This is an extremely important topic. Christian Answers reported, "Larry King, the CNN talk show host, was once asked who he would most want to interview if he could choose anyone from all of history. He said, 'Jesus Christ.' The questioner said, 'And what would you like to ask Him?' King replied, 'I would like to ask Him if He was indeed virgin-born. The answer to that question would define history for me.'"

Who would you like to meet from history? Why?

_____
_____
_____

What would you ask them?

_____
_____
_____

Isaiah 7:14 records this amazing miracle, **"Therefore the Lord himself will give you a sign. Behold, the virgin shall conceive and bear a son, and shall call his name Immanuel."** Never before did the words **"virgin"** and **"conceive"** coincide. Conceive implies that she is no longer a virgin.

N. T. Wright observed, "First-century folk knew every bit as well as we do that babies are produced by sexual intercourse. When, in Matthew's version of the story, Joseph heard about Mary's pregnancy, his problem arose not because he didn't know the facts of life, but because he did."

179

LESSON EIGHT JESUS WAS SINLESS

Were your parents comfortable talking about "the birds and the bees?"

_____

_____

_____

There is a tendency or movement within our "Christian" society to downplay the virgin birth. J.A. Medders listed seven questions to ask anyone who does not believe the virgin birth was important.

Jesus was, or was not, miraculously placed in Mary's womb by the Holy Spirit?

If he was not, why would Matthew (Matthew 1:18–25) and Luke (Luke 1:26–38) say so? Are they liars or hype-men for Jesus?

If Jesus was not born of the Virgin Mary, how did the eternal Son of God enter this world?

If he was not virgin-born, when and where did the divine nature of the man Jesus come from? Joseph's sperm? Mary's egg? Or the divine nature Jesus always had from eternity, via the virgin birth?

If Jesus was not divinely placed in Mary's womb, it was an ordinary conception—normal fertilization—do you think Jesus became God at some point? What other option is there?

If Jesus was not placed in Mary's womb by the Spirit, how is Jesus free from the stain of Adam's sin? Without the virgin birth, we don't have a sinless substitute, we have no atonement, and we have no resurrection.

LESSON EIGHT JESUS WAS SINLESS

Why pick one miracle over another? Why believe in a dead man coming back to life, never dying again, and reigning over the Universe—and not the virgin birth?

John F. MacArthur, Jr. adds, "The virgin birth is an underlying assumption of everything the Bible says about Jesus. To throw out the virgin birth is to reject Christ's deity, the accuracy and authority of Scripture, and a host of other related doctrines that are the heart of the Christian faith. No issue is more important than the virgin birth to our understanding of who Jesus is. If we deny Jesus is God, we have denied the very essence of Christianity."

Jesus was not born with a sin nature. From the start, He was perfect. Every day He chose to keep it that way. Scripture is very clear that He never sinned. If He had sinned, He could not be the sacrificial lamb for us.

Going By Faith lists ten sins that people often overlook or accept in their daily walk.

1. Holding grudges
2. Justifying wrong attitudes
3. Putting your desires first (before God)
4. Feeling annoyed over the success of others
5. Getting hurt easily and reacting out of the hurt
6. Underpaying (taking advantage of others' work)
7. Skimping on the work you are being paid to do
8. Criticizing and finding fault — secretly or outwardly
9. Focusing on the cares of the world — putting your full attention and trust in the "things" of the world, like money, power, possessions, and image. When we allow that to define us, we lose focus of who we are in Christ. This does not mean not caring about what happens in the world.
10. Gossiping or speaking unkindly of those not present

LESSON EIGHT JESUS WAS SINLESS

Are all of these sins?

_____

_____

_____

Which is most common?

_____

_____

_____

The Bible is very clear about Jesus living a perfect life. He never sinned through inappropriate actions. He never sinned with inappropriate words. He never sinned with inappropriate thoughts. He never sinned!

Peter writes in 1 Peter 2:22, *"He committed no sin, neither was deceit found in his mouth."*

Who is this verse discussing?

_____

_____

_____

Paul writes in 2 Corinthians 5:21, *"For our sake he made him to be sin who knew no sin, so that in him we might become the righteousness of God."*

What does this verse mean?

_____

_____

_____

LESSON EIGHT JESUS WAS SINLESS

The author of Hebrews writes (4:15), *"For we do not have a high priest who is unable to sympathize with our weaknesses, but one who in every respect has been tempted as we are, yet without sin."*

How are temptation and sin different from each other?

_____

_____

_____

John writes in 1 John 3:5, *"You know that he appeared in order to take away sins, and in him there is no sin."*

Why did Jesus come to earth?

_____

_____

_____

Why is it important that *"in him there is no sin?"*

_____

_____

_____

John 19:4 Pilate went out again and said to them, *"See, I am bringing him out to you that you may know that I find no guilt in him."*

How many different people recorded that Jesus was sinless?

_____

_____

_____

183

LESSON EIGHT JESUS WAS SINLESS

Isaiah 53:9 contains valuable prophecy, *"And they made his grave with the wicked and with a rich man in his death, although he had done no violence, and there was no deceit in his mouth."*

How was Jesus' grave with the wicked?

_____

_____

_____

How was Jesus' death with a rich man?

_____

_____

_____

What else does this prophecy say about Jesus (the Messiah)?

_____

_____

_____

1 Peter 1:18-19 *"Knowing that you were ransomed from the futile ways inherited from your forefathers, not with perishable things such as silver or gold, but with the precious blood of Christ, like that of a lamb without blemish or spot."*

How is Jesus described here?

_____

_____

_____

James 4:17 takes sin to a whole different level, *"So whoever knows the right thing to do and fails to do it, for him it is sin."*

184

LESSON EIGHT JESUS WAS SINLESS

What are some sins of commission?

_____

_____

_____

In talking about the impeccability (whether or not Jesus could sin) of Christ, Charles C. Ryrie describes both sides, "One says that He was able not to sin while the other states that He was not able to sin. In either case He did not sin."

Jesus did not sin; therefore, He could and did die for our sins. Thank you, Jesus!

LESSON EIGHT JESUS WAS SINLESS

JOHN 19:4

JESUS WAS SINLESS, DEVOTION 1
Ryan Story | *Student Pastor*

We all know that critical person who can find something wrong in every situation. We all know the person who will say it is too hot or too cold outside. You know that person who is unhappy if their food takes too long to get to their table. They are the person who can spot cobwebs from fifty feet away and say that an entire room is filthy. We all know that person who is more focused on their preference than principles. Sadly, we all have moments of being critical, we all have the pet-peeves that drive us crazy. Think of the way we start to treat people when they do not live up to our expectations. If a waiter takes too long to deliver food, we instantly jump to the conclusion that they are out to get us. We are so quick to find fault with people. Even worse, we are quick to finding fault with God as well.

In John chapter 19, Jesus is in the middle of a very bad night. The Pharisee leaders arrested Jesus. Now they want to put Jesus to death, but they cannot because they lack any true governing power. To execute Jesus, the Pharisees just need to get the Roman prefect to say this execution was just. John 19:4 says, ***"Pilate went out again and said to them, 'See, I am bringing him out to you that you may know that I find no guilt in him.'"*** After meeting and questioning Jesus, Pilate was not able to find any fault in Jesus of Nazareth. It amazes me that Pilate was able to look at this Jewish man and see no guilt in Him. Pilate was a Roman leader who was doing his best to keep Jerusalem under control so he would not lose his job and life for failing the Roman Empire. To me, the easiest thing Pilate could have done in this situation would be to do what we all

187

JESUS WAS SINLESS DEVOTION 1

try to do, find a fault when one is not there. Amazingly, Pilate could not find anything to say showing Jesus was guilty.

Any Christ follower will agree with you that Jesus is God. He was sinless, perfect, and without any worldly blemish. Knowing that Jesus is the only person who we can say is perfect is such a peaceful feeling. Knowing that all of God's ways are perfect, sinless, loving, merciful, and just should be at the central hub of our faith. Then why is it that when our situations in life are not where they should be, one of the first people we want to find fault in is God? Pilate examined Jesus for a substantial amount of time and found no fault in Him, and he was not even aware that Jesus was, in fact, the Christ, the world's Savior, the King of kings. We are aware of all those things, and yet we still think God is unfair when there is turmoil in our families, a tragedy strikes, or when finances are not as bountiful as we were hoping. If we know that Jesus is, in fact, perfect and sinless, then His plan for our lives must be the same. Too often I hear people who think that difficult situations in life mean that God is not real, perfect, or just. Instead of looking for the problem in the One who is in control, look at how you can change your perspective. God is perfect and sinless. His plan is perfect. Take a page out of a Roman's life, view God as without guilt, without fault, and perfect in all He does.

1 PETER 1:18-19

JESUS WAS SINLESS, DEVOTION 2
James Clouse | *Student Pastor*

Have you ever given your children a spit shine? If you do not know what this is, a spit shine is when you have a child with a spot of dirt or food on them, and you lick a rag or your finger to rub the spot off your child. Lorelai, my daughter, hates spit shines. Every time I go to do it now, she complains and says for me just to leave it, but I have to make sure she is clean and presentable before others.

Jesus, has in a sense, given us a spit shine. Christ has taken every blemish and spot of sin and cleaned it off of us to make us clean and presentable before His Father.

1 Peter 1:18-19 says, ***"Knowing that you were ransomed from the futile ways inherited from your forefathers, not with perishable things such as silver or gold, but with the precious blood of Christ, like that of a lamb without blemish or spot."***

Christ has taken our futile sins and every blemish and cleaned them with His blood. As human beings, we were born into a world of sin, into a world where it is impossible to remain perfect and without blemish. These sins were inherited, which means that this is our nature. We were born into it and given it by our fathers and their fathers before them.

There is only one way that we can be cleansed of these blemishes, and that is through Jesus Christ. First Peter points out that we cannot be saved by perishable things such as silver or gold. We

JESUS WAS SINLESS DEVOTION 2

cannot buy or earn our way into Heaven. Things of this Earth are not good enough to redeem us before our Father.

When I die, the Father will not see me but the precious blood of His Son who died for us. This is what redeems us. All of the sins of my past and in my life are placed at the cross. We have been sanctified through Christ and what He did for us. We are made perfect, clean, and presentable before our Father.

1 PETER 2:22

JESUS WAS SINLESS, DEVOTION 3
Caleb Combs | *Gathering Pastor*

Jesus was a lamb without spot, a perfect sacrifice. In the book of Exodus, you find the children of Israel enslaved by the Egyptians. They were in a place and an experience that God had never designed for His people. Ultimately, God planned to get His people to turn back to Him, trust Him, and He would lead them to the Promised Land. The Bible tells us in Exodus 1 that He heard the cries of His people.

God used a man named Moses to lead His people back to Him. Now it would not be an easy or uneventful Exodus because the Egyptians needed the Israelites. God told Moses to go in front of Pharaoh and tell him he would inflict ten plagues on the land. It included removing their water source, bugs, and boils, to fiery hail and darkness. God was trying to get their attention. However, it was not until the tenth and final plague that Pharaoh released the Israelites. The tenth plague was called the Passover. God instructed Moses in Exodus chapter 12, that an angel would come over the land and kill the firstborn of every family. The only way the angel would pass over a home is if the blood of a lamb or goat was spread across the doorway of the home. The Bible describes the lamb needed in Exodus 12:5, *"Your lamb shall be without blemish, a male a year old. You may take it from the sheep or from the goats."*

Why would the lamb need to be without blemish? One opinion is that God deserves and requires our best and if we decide we do not want to give Him our best, we are relying on our self. Another

JESUS WAS SINLESS DEVOTION 3

concept is summarized in a quote by Gerald Bray, "If the lamb were less than perfect, someone might say it was being sacrificed because of its defects, but that is not true. It was not the lamb that was the problem but for those whom the lamb was dying."

We see the need for a lamb's blood for protection for the Israelites during the Passover and is a perfect picture for our lives. The Perfect Lamb (Jesus) was slain, and His blood was the covering of our sin. It is not on our merit or status that we are saved, but by the blood of the Perfect Lamb. The lamb was not the problem and would not be needed except for what is said in Hebrews 9:22, *"Indeed, under the law almost everything is purified with blood, and without the shedding of blood there is no forgiveness of sins."* Jesus was the perfect sacrifice needed to cover our faults and failures, and He willingly stepped in on our behalf. 1 Peter 2:22 says, *"He committed no sin, neither was deceit found in his mouth."*

1 JOHN 3:5

JESUS WAS SINLESS, DEVOTION 4
Jayson Combs | *Family Pastor*

When I was in the eleventh grade, I did something that forever marked my life. It is something I carried around with me every day since. It took place in my sixth-hour class. I accidentally stabbed myself in the arm with a number 2 pencil. It is not like it hurt that bad, but now I have this blemish on my arm that for 20 years is still going strong. It is this little lead dot on my arm (I know it is not lead). If you are my age or older there is a good chance that you have one of these blemishes (if you are younger, you may not know what a pencil is).

In 1 John 3:2-6 it says, *"Beloved, we are God's children now, and what we will be has not yet appeared; but we know that when he appears we shall be like him, because we shall see him as he is. And everyone who thus hopes in him purifies himself as he is pure. Everyone who makes a practice of sinning also practices lawlessness; sin is lawlessness. You know that he appeared in order to take away sins, and in him there is no sin. No one who abides in him keeps on sinning; no one who keeps on sinning has either seen him or known him."*

It says that we who hope in Him are purified because He (Jesus) is pure. The word pure means to be "free from contamination," to be free from blemish. Verse five goes on to say that Jesus came to *"take away sins, and in Him there is no sin."* The Bible defines sin many different ways: *"Whosoever is not of faith is sin"* (Romans 14:23 KJV), *"The thought of foolishness is sin"* (Proverbs 24:9 KJV), *"Therefore to him that knoweth to do good and doeth it*

JESUS WAS SINLESS DEVOTION 4

not to him it is sin" (James 4:17), *"All unrighteousness is sin"* (1 John 5:17 KJV), and the *"practice of sinning also practices lawlessness"* (1 John 3:2).

The Word of God points out our sin. That is precisely what the Law of the Old Testament was to do. It was to show us all that we all fall short; we are all blemished. Without one who is perfect, we are all lost and condemned. There is only one who has no blemish. He is the one, and the only one, that could set us free from sin. Jesus, my Lord and Savior, is pure without blemish, in Him, there is no contamination. In Him, I have freedom and the forgiveness of sin.

2 CORINTHIANS 5:21

JESUS WAS SINLESS, DEVOTION 5
Chuck Lindsey | *Reach Pastor*

"*For He made Him who knew no sin to be sin for us, that we might become the righteousness of God in Him.*" 2 Corinthians 5:21 (NKJV)

From the earliest age, I remember having dominoes. Not the pizza (although that sounds pretty good right now), but the game. I must confess, that in all the years I have had a dominoes' set, though they got a lot of use, I have never actually played the game of dominoes. How did I use them? Do you already know? That is right; I spent hours carefully standing them up into lines, circles, and paths only to knock the first one over and watch them with expectation as each one fell one after another. Did you know there are domino toppling competitions? It is a thing, and it is mesmerizing to watch. Teams of people spend days (sometimes weeks) carefully setting every domino at just the right distance and angle from each other, so that when the first domino is knocked over each of the thousands of succeeding dominoes fall as expected. The current world record is almost 4.5 million dominoes. Incredible! The "domino effect" is a phrase that was coined from this phenomenon and it describes a "chain reaction" between objects or ideas. Doctrine is like dominoes. One truth builds on another. If you knock one over it causes a chain reaction "down the line" as it were. It has become popular of late for "Christian" leaders/writers to question and dismiss clear and established doctrine. Among those beliefs has been the doctrine of the Virgin Birth.

When we say, "the Virgin Birth" we are talking about the birth of Jesus Christ. The Bible teaches that Jesus was not conceived through the

JESUS WAS SINLESS DEVOTION 5

physical union of a man and a woman. We are told instead, that God "overshadowed" the woman, meaning that He "placed" His Son, the Savior of the world, into the womb of the yet unmarried virgin named Mary. Jesus was conceived by God and born of the woman. This is what the Bible (God) says happened.

Now, this is an essential doctrinal "domino." Why? Because, if Jesus had been conceived through "human means," He could have only ever been that, human. He would have been no more than we are. But He is infinitely more than just a human being. He is both man and God at the same time. As the Puritans said it, "He is all of man and all of very God" meaning that Jesus is 100% man and 100% God at the same time. You say, "wait, is that not 200%?" Yes, that is why I said He is more!

You see because Jesus was born both of the woman and of God, He stands alone in all of history. He is the "God-Man." As such, He stands in the middle, between both God and man. He is, as the Scriptures say, *"the Mediator between God and men"* (1 Timothy 2:5 NKJV). He alone holds this place because He alone is both God and man at the same time.

Now, if you knock that domino over, and deny His Virgin Birth, then a chain reaction occurs and other dominoes fall. To deny He was virgin born (domino #1) means that He is not God (domino #2) and thus could not be sinless (domino #3). That means that He cannot die as the "sinless substitute" for our sins (domino #4) which then means that we are still in our sins and unsaved (domino #5). Ultimately, Christianity is a false hope (the last domino to fall).

However, if He really was conceived of God and born of the virgin, then He is both God and man and 2 Corinthians 5:21 (NKJV) is a shout of victory: *"For He* (the Father) *made Him* (Jesus) *who knew no sin* (He was sinless, innocent) *to be sin for us* (He took our sins on Himself), *that we might become the righteousness of God* (innocent) *in Him."* The sinless One, the innocent One, our Savior, the Lord Jesus, did not need to die for His sins, He had none (domino #1). He took our sin on Himself (domino #2) and died in our place (domino #3) so that we could become innocent through Him (domino #4) and thus we are truly saved. What sweet dominoes fall as we trust the truth of what God has said.

JESUS WAS SINLESS DEVOTION 5

HEBREWS 4:15

JESUS WAS SINLESS, DEVOTION 6
Joshua Combs | *Lead Pastor*

"For we do not have a high priest who is unable to sympathize with our weaknesses, but one who in every respect has been tempted as we are, yet without sin." Hebrews 4:15

What a wonderful joy it is to know that in our temptations we are not alone! In both the Gospel of Matthew and Luke, we see Jesus face a barrage of temptations from the enemy. Satan attacks Jesus with three distinct evil schemes (1 John 2:16 calls them, *"The desires of the flesh and the desires of the eyes and pride of life."*) and each time the Lord repels the volleys of the Devil. What is crucial to understand is that Jesus faced each type of temptation that we will ever face, demonstrating for us how to defeat temptation. An important promise that God has made to us concerning temptation is found in 1Corinthians 10:13. The Scripture reads, *"No temptation has overtaken you that is not common to man. God is faithful, and He will not let you be tempted beyond your ability, but with the temptation He will also provide the way of escape, that you may be able to endure it."* Jesus not only gives us the battle plans for overcoming temptation, but empowers us, through the Holy Spirit, to endure the fiery trials of temptation.

Another profound principle we learn from the temptation of Christ is that to be tempted is not sin. Jesus was led by the Holy Spirit into the wilderness to be tempted (Mathew 4:1), but He remained *"without sin."* When we face temptation or our flesh (see Galatians 5:16-25) desires something evil, the devil will use guilt to make us

JESUS WAS SINLESS DEVOTION 6

feel defeated, but we must realize to face temptation is not sin. We must endure and look urgently for the way of escape that God has promised to provide. The promised escape hatch is there. Find it. Take it! Know that Jesus sympathizes with our human weaknesses (Hebrews 4:15), He has paved the way for escape, and empowers us to take the way of escape. Sometimes fleeing temptation (2 Timothy 2:22) will be mental, sometimes that means physically leaving where you are, changing media habits, or altering your driving patterns.

Whatever temptation tactic Satan attacks you with, know that Jesus faces that temptation with you!

JESUS WAS SINLESS DEVOTION 6

201

09

JESUS DIED
FOR OUR SINS

DR. RANDY T. JOHNSON,
GROWTH PASTOR

LESSON NINE JESUS DIED FOR OUR SINS

Jon Gordon wrote a fascinating book, *"No Complaining Rule: Positive Ways to Deal with Negativity."* The main premise of the book is that people should come with solutions, not just problems. Too often people feel they have the "gift of criticism" and they take no responsibility in resolving the issue. Gordon noted that this negativity was slowly killing organizations. He demanded that when people see a problem, they go one step further than just reporting it (or whining); he proposed they find a way to make it right or at least better.

How do you deal with negativity?

_____

_____

_____

Who are a few of the most encouraging people you know?

_____

_____

_____

Finding a solution for the problem is heroic.

There are 1,189 chapters in the Bible. In the third chapter of the Bible, we have a huge problem. The problem is that man sinned against God and broke the relationship with Him. This was a major dilemma. There was nothing man could do. God realized there was nothing man could do. So, in the same chapter, God presents a solution. God made a plan. He had the "fix" for the broken relationship. It was the death of Jesus.

First, it is important to realize from Scripture that man has a problem. The problem is called sin.

203

LESSON NINE JESUS DIED FOR OUR SINS

Why is sin a problem?

_____

_____

_____

Problem - Man's sin

David sinned in many ways. He was lazy, irresponsible, lustful, an adulterous, and even a murderer. He wrote Psalm chapter 32 and chapter 51 expressing his godly remorse. Psalm 51:5 says, ***"Behold, I was brought forth in iniquity, and in sin did my mother conceive me."*** David not only sinned as an adult, he realized that his problem and our problem is much bigger than that; we were born sinners.

What does it mean that we are born with a sin nature?

_____

_____

_____

What "sins" do you see in little children that were not "taught" to them?

_____

_____

_____

Romans 3:10-12 says, ***"As it is written: 'None is righteous, no, not one; no one understands; no one seeks for God. All have turned aside; together they have become worthless; no one does good, not even one."***

How many times do these verses express our problem?

_____

_____

_____

204

LESSON NINE JESUS DIED FOR OUR SINS

Romans 3:23 continues the desperate need for help, *"For all have sinned and fall short of the glory of God."*

What does it mean to *"fall short of the glory of God?"*

_____

_____

_____

Jeremiah 17:9 paints an interesting picture, *"The heart is deceitful above all things, and desperately sick; who can understand it?"*

Is it good to just "follow your heart?"

_____

_____

_____

Galatians 5:17 says, *"For the desires of the flesh are against the Spirit, and the desires of the Spirit are against the flesh, for these are opposed to each other, to keep you from doing the things you want to do."*

What is meant by *"the flesh"* and *"the Spirit?"*

_____

_____

_____

Ecclesiastes 7:20 adds, *"Surely there is not a righteous man on earth who does good and never sins."*

How many different books of the Bible listed here show our problem?

_____

_____

_____

205

LESSON NINE JESUS DIED FOR OUR SINS

Sin was and is our problem. The solution was and is that Jesus died for our sins.

D.A. Carson said, "It was not nails that held Jesus to that wretched cross; it was his unqualified resolution, out of love for his Father, to do his Father's will—and it was his love for sinners like me."

Solution - Jesus died for our sins

C. S. Lewis said, "It costs God nothing, so far as we know, to create nice things; but to convert rebellious wills cost Him crucifixion." God created everything out of nothing with just a spoken word. However, to correct a problem, cost Him everything.

Paul wrote in 1 Corinthians 15:3, *"For I delivered to you as of first importance what I also received: that Christ died for our sins in accordance with the Scriptures."*

What is meant by *"of first importance?"*

_____

_____

1 Peter 3:18 *"For Christ also suffered once for sins, the righteous for the unrighteous, that he might bring us to God, being put to death in the flesh but made alive in the spirit."*

According to this verse, why did Jesus suffer?

_____

_____

_____

LESSON NINE JESUS DIED FOR OUR SINS

Romans 5:6 *"For while we were still weak, at the right time Christ died for the ungodly." Verse 8 adds, "But God shows his love for us in that while we were still sinners, Christ died for us."*

What was our state when Jesus died for us?

How good do we have to become before accepting the grace of God?

Mark 10:45 *"For even the Son of Man came not to be served but to serve, and to give his life as a ransom for many."*

What does the word *"ransom"* mean and how does that relate to the topic?

According to this verse, why did Jesus come to earth?

"God proved His love on the Cross. When Christ hung, and bled, and died, it was God saying to the world, 'I love you.'" Billy Graham

207

LESSON NINE JESUS DIED FOR OUR SINS

ROMANS 3:10-12

JESUS DIED FOR OUR SINS, DEVOTION 1
Ryan Story | *Student Pastor*

Why do bad things happen to good people?

In August of 2015, a family member's life was taken. He got himself caught up in a really bad situation, and another person took my cousin's life. This was hard for my family and me. For a period, I became close to him. During his funeral the "pastor" overseeing the funeral started with "sometimes bad things, tragic things happen to good people." The moment this man said that a cold chill went through my soul. The majority of the people in this funeral were non-believers. I listened as a "man of God" got up and told an entire room that my cousin was a "good" person only to use Psalm chapter 23 as a reference point.

I understand that comforting and mourning with those who are hurting during a funeral is one of the primary responsibilities of a Pastor during a funeral. The other major responsibility is speaking the truth. We live in such a hard, cold, cynical culture, but our culture also is terrified to offend people. Now I am not speaking ill of my cousin, but he was not a good person. I am not a good person. You reading this, you are not a good person. Every human who is alive is not a good person. We all have sinned. We all have this inherited inward disposition to rebel against our God. Hearing a person say "bad things happen to good people" out of the mouth of a man who is meant to preach the Good News of Jesus Christ was nothing more than hurting the people who were listening.

In the book of Romans chapter 3, Paul puts every Jewish Christian and every Gentile Christian reader in the same box. Paul places

JESUS DIED FOR OUR SINS DEVOTION 1

every person into "the box of sin." Romans 3:10-12 says, ***"None is righteous, no, not one; no one understands; no one seeks for God. All have turned aside; together they have become worthless; no one does good, not even one."*** We have already covered that God's Word is perfect and absolute earlier in this Majors Series. To have the Bible say that no one is righteous, no one seeks God, all have turned aside, and no one does good is an absolute truth. The only person to be born of a woman who was born good was Jesus, for the rest of us, we fall into the fourteen indictments that Paul places on all of humanity in the book of Romans. The grim, cold truth is there is no such thing as a good person except for Jesus.

Man's sinfulness is plainly seen in any act of abuse, violence, neglect, envy, and anger. Those are easy for us to recognize. It is when we start to create our sense of what is "good" is when we get into trouble. The moment we stop using God's way as the measuring stick to what is good or bad, we are in trouble. In God's eye, glancing at a woman in lust is adultery. Being angry because someone cut you off in traffic is the same as you purposely, mercilessly murdering him or her. To answer the age-old, "why do bad things happen to good people," my response is generally, "Show me a good person." This thought is not meant to be depressing; it should be uplifting knowing we are all on the same playing field in God's creation. No matter how "not good" we are, He still loves us, and loved us so much He sent His son to die for us.

ROMANS 3:23

JESUS DIED FOR OUR SINS, DEVOTION 2
Tommy Youngquist | *Children's Pastor*

I hate going to see a doctor! I always think to myself, "This will pass, and I will be fine," no matter what it is. If I am sick, I never think that what I have is worth the trip, effort, and time it takes to see the doctor. Most of the time the doctor just tells you what you already know and charges you a fee to do so. Therefore, I am usually miserable until whatever I have "passes." Can any of you relate to this type of thinking? Am I the only one?

This type of thinking reminds me of how the natural man views sin. Sin is not a problem to them. Human nature is not viewed as a bad thing. "There is nothing wrong with me, and I do not need a doctor," they think to themselves. Why try to fix something if you do not think it is broke, right? The problem is that all of humanity is sick and in need of a doctor. We are debilitated with our selfishness.

Romans 3:23 says, *"For all have sinned and fall short of the glory of God."*

The first step towards fixing any problem is recognizing that there is a problem. Jesus said in Luke 5:31-32, *"Those who are well have no need of a physician, but those who are sick. I have not come to call the righteous but sinners to repentance."* Once you realize you have a problem, you will be more apt to let someone fix it. This is our problem: All have sinned! All of humanity has been branded with sin. I have sinned (and still do). You sin. We have a sickness, a sickness that is destroying us. When we realize this, we allow God the opportunity to fix us.

JESUS DIED FOR OUR SINS DEVOTION 2

When we come to the point of realization about our sin, humble ourselves, and repent of our sin, Jesus starts to work in our lives. He starts to heal our brokenness. He begins to remedy our sickness. He waits for us to come to Him. He is always there for us, too. Unlike the doctor, He does not charge us a fee to tell us what we already know. He paid the price!

COLOSSIANS 2:13-14

JESUS DIED FOR OUR SINS, DEVOTION 3
Jayson Combs | *Family Pastor*

What is a sin? Have you sinned before? These are the questions that I often ask when speaking to children in regards to salvation. This question must be answered for us to move on in regards to salvation. Colossians 2:13 says, *"And you, who were dead in your trespasses."* The word trespasses can also be translated as sin. It is a pretty straightforward statement - because of sin, we are dead.

Recently, I had the opportunity to visit the country of Israel. While we were there, we made a stop at the Dead Sea. Driving along the sea was amazing. The blue water with the mountains reflecting off the water is breathtaking. As you get closer, you realize why they call it the Dead Sea. There is no life in and around the Dead Sea. It is just desert, sand, salt, and rocks. It is hard for me to imagine this huge body of water having zero life in it - no fish, no plants, nothing. It is pretty, but it is dead.

This is the picture of our lives without Jesus. We can have a pretty outside, but without the saving grace of Jesus, we are dead. I am so happy that verse 13 does not stop there. The rest of this passage goes on to say, *"God made alive together with him, having forgiven us all our trespasses, by canceling the record of debt that stood against us with its legal demands. This he set aside, nailing it to the cross."*

If you grew up in church, and especially in a youth group, you most likely had a service where you nailed a piece of paper to a cross.

JESUS DIED FOR OUR SINS DEVOTION 3

Usually, what happens is the speaker at the end of his lesson tells the students that they can take their piece of paper and write any sins on the paper. Then they are invited to come up to a cross and nail that paper to it. That symbolic event comes from this passage of Scripture. It is the picture of what Jesus does for us on the cross. The debt of sin that all of us carry can only be forgiven when they are taken to the cross. Jesus came so our sins could be forgiven. We no longer live in death when we confess Him as Lord and Savior, but in life and eternity.

GALATIANS 5:17

JESUS DIED FOR OUR SINS, DEVOTION 4
Caleb Combs | *Gathering Pastor*

We all remember growing up and watching cartoons. Some of us still enjoy watching them. Remember the cartoon character that comes across a situation where he must decide to do right or wrong? The cartoon then showed us a memorable picture. At that moment, an angel appeared on his right shoulder and began to "influence" him to do right. Then out of nowhere, a devil appeared on the other shoulder with a deep raspy voice and attempted to convince the character to do wrong. The cartoonist painted a picture with visuals, but also characteristics. The characteristics of the good angel showed him wearing white, put together in appearance, and with a very soft weak voice. The devil, on the other hand, was the exact opposite of the "good" angel. He had horns and wore a red cape, yielded a pitchfork, and had a strong, deep voice. These two characters would argue and battle back and forth for the next few minutes, attempting to convince the cartoon character to go to their side and do what they wanted. This battle, although funny in a cartoon, is a great picture of the innermost beings of every follower of Christ.

Of course, we do not have two little cartoons that appear on our shoulders every time we need to make a decision, but we have two innate sides that fight for influence in our life every single day. The Bible calls them Spirit (good) and Flesh (bad). When we are born into the world, we are born into the flesh. Because of Adam's sin, we are all now born into sin. Romans 3:23 tells us, ***"All have sinned and fall short of the glory of God."*** You see, God created man perfect, but in our failure, we brought the flesh into our lives. Through the

JESUS DIED FOR OUR SINS DEVOTION 4

cross and blood of Jesus, we gain access to the Spirit. It is only when we repent of our sins and call upon the name of the Lord to be our Savior, that we receive the Spirit in our lives. However, we still battle the flesh. How do we balance the two? Galatians 5:17 tells us, *"For the desires of the flesh are against the Spirit, and the desires of the Spirit are against the flesh, for these are opposed to each other, to keep you from doing the things you want to do."* Although we laugh at the picture drawn in the cartoons, it is a real battle that rages every day inside us. The key to fighting the battle between flesh and spirit is paying attention to which side we are feeding.

We can feed the spirit by reading God's Word. His Word is our daily bread; it is nourishment to our souls. We need to be constantly growing in His Word to feed the Spirit. We need to spend time with God in prayer, constantly seeking His direction in our lives. The Bible is a perfect blueprint for living in the Spirit. I love the acronym for the Bible, "Believers Instruction Before Leaving Earth." The more we feed the Spirit in our lives, the more it grows and influences our decisions. However, the same goes for the flesh. The more we feed the flesh, the bigger it gets and the more it influences our decisions. We feed the flesh by ignoring the Bible and its teachings and doing whatever is contrary to what God says.

As a believer, we have to understand this battle wages inside us, because if you do not realize it, you could be feeding the flesh and block out the spirit in your life. The Apostle Paul warns his listeners in 1 Thessalonians 5:14-19 not to *"quench the Spirit."* Man is that a scary thought! I cringe at the thought of blocking out or quenching God's direction in my life.

Which are you feeding more? What changes do you need to make to start feeding the Spirit? Have you been feeding the flesh for so

JESUS DIED FOR OUR SINS DEVOTION 4

long that it has grown so large you cannot even hear the Spirit? Today is the day to seek God's will and direction in your life and begin feeding the Spirit. You and I need to get to it!

JESUS DIED FOR OUR SINS DEVOTION 4

JEREMIAH 17:9

JESUS DIED FOR OUR SINS, DEVOTION 5
Chuck Lindsey | *Reach Pastor*

"The heart is deceitful above all things, and desperately sick; who can understand it?" Jeremiah 17:9

Have you ever given or been advised to "just follow your heart?" Have you heard the encouragement that "you cannot go wrong if you just listen to your heart?" According to the Bible, that might not be the best idea. While many may believe and teach that the heart is an infallible guide, God says quite the opposite. Listen to His words about the heart.

In Jeremiah 17:9, God says that the human heart (another word for the inward life of a person) *"is deceitful."* The word "deceitful" there means that it is tricky, not sure-footed, and polluted. Wow! That is pretty strong language God uses to describe what so many others describe in flowery terms. God does not stop there. He says that the human heart is not only *"deceitful"* but that it is "trickery" or it can fool us *"above all things."* Wait a minute, is God telling us that our heart is more deceitful than anything else in life? Yep! How can this be? Think about it; your heart is inside you. Your "heart" describes your inward life. All your thoughts, emotions, and being are all summed up in the word "heart." When you consider that, then it makes sense why the "heart" has this ability to so effectively trick us. God says something else, something shocking about the human heart. He says that it is *"desperately sick."* These words mean "incurably sick." He then says, *"who can understand it?"* This means that even we cannot know our own heart completely.

219

JESUS DIED FOR OUR SINS DEVOTION 5

All of this leads to a couple of conclusions:

The heart is not a trustworthy guide. Right? I mean, if God says it is incurably sick, cannot be known, and tricks us more than anything else does, there can only be one conclusion. It is not a reliable guide. This means that the "way we feel" about something cannot be our guide for what is true and what is not. It also cannot be the "compass" we use for navigating the rough waters of life.

Man is a sinner. If the "heart" is the word used to describe the entire inward life of a person. Then it describes us. It describes us at our "core." In short, to say the heart is like this is to say that we are like this (apart from Christ). Consider what God is saying, "the entire inward life of a person (all their thoughts, affections, emotions and will) apart from Me, are deceiving them above all things. They are incurably sick, and they do not even know it." Yikes!

It is because of this that Jesus came to die. When you consider what God says about the human heart, one thing becomes clear; man was not ever going to fix himself. Man was not ever going to dig himself out of his sinful state. Man was not going to figure it out. We were not getting better throughout the ages with all of our "advancements," we were only getting worse. So, God came to rescue us. Because we could not rescue ourselves, "Christ died for our sins according to the Scriptures." It is only as the Holy Spirit of God convicts a person of their total sinful condition and convinces them of the truth of the Gospel and Jesus' ability to save, that a person can become a ***"new creation in Christ Jesus"*** and sing, *"Amazing grace how sweet the sound to save a wretch like me. I once was lost but now I am found, was blind but now I see."*

220

ECCLESIASTES 7:20

JESUS DIED FOR OUR SINS, DEVOTION 6
Joshua Combs | *Lead Pastor*

"Surely *there is not a righteous man on earth who does good and never sins."* Ecclesiastes 7:20

If you have ever shared the Gospel or engaged in a spiritual conversation before, one of the most common discussions will center around how we get to Heaven and who gets to go to Heaven. Several years ago, I was given a counseling referral to meet with a mother and her daughters. The mother was a professing Christian whose daughters were extremely skeptical and, honestly, somewhat hostile towards Christianity. The mother's goal, unbeknownst to me when we began, was for me, the pastor, to convince the daughters of, not only the validity of Christianity but the very existence of God. It was no small order! What transpired in my office over the next hour, was one of the most disturbing meetings I have ever experienced. Frankly, I have been haunted by it ever since. I began by asking some questions, attempting to grasp the worldview that these young ladies and their mother held. I quickly realized that I was dealing with an extremely humanistic viewpoint. I talked about creation, the historical evidence of the existence and ministry of Jesus, and the validity of the Bible as we know it. Up to this point, the Mom was completely on my side. But I knew at the core, what was needed was a faithful presentation of the Gospel and, Lord willing, the conversion of these students. As I began to turn the conversation from several extremely hot-button cultural issues to the Gospel, I could not have anticipated what would happen. Every faithful presentation of the Gospel begins with a fundamental understanding that we are sinners and in need of a savior. Romans

JESUS DIED FOR OUR SINS DEVOTION 6

3:11 says, *"None is righteous, no, not one... all have sinned and fall short of the glory of God."* There are no exceptions. Everyone ever born has sinned against God and needs to be saved from their sin. As I shared Romans 3, not only were these two girls disgusted at the proclamation from Scripture that everyone not only sins, but is innately sinful, but their mother began to adamantly disagree that everyone sins and cannot save themselves. That is where this meeting came to a screeching halt.

Unless someone realizes their absolute helplessness in the light of sin and that condition encompasses the whole of mankind, there is simply no way to go forward with the Gospel. You cannot get to the Good News until there is an acceptance of the bad news. As that meeting came to an end, my heart broke. Not only were these two young, intelligent girls lost in sin, but their mother did not understand the true Gospel either.

The total sinful depravity of man is a fundamental truth of Christianity. We are, as the Bible says, *"dead in the trespasses and sins"* (Ephesians 2:1). We are not kind of dead. We are not on spiritual life support. We are utterly and hopelessly lost in sin. We are slaves to sin. But Jesus came. He died for our sins. He did not just come and die to be a personal improvement program or establish a superior religious movement. Jesus was the only means of salvation. His atoning work on the cross of Calvary is the only means of salvation and freedom from our sin.

JESUS DIED FOR OUR SINS DEVOTION 6

10

JESUS ROSE AGAIN & THE ASCENSION

DR. RANDY T. JOHNSON, GROWTH PASTOR

LESSON TEN JESUS ROSE AGAIN & THE ASCENSION

" I checked the tomb of Buddha, and it was occupied, and I checked the tomb of Confucius and it was occupied, and I checked the tomb of Mohammed and it was occupied, and I came to the tomb of Jesus and it was empty. And I said, There is one who conquered death." John MacArthur

Jesus is alive!

Charles Colson said, "I know the resurrection is a fact, and Watergate proved it to me. How? Because 12 men testified they had seen Jesus raised from the dead, then they proclaimed that truth for 40 years, never once denying it. Every one was beaten, tortured, stoned and put in prison. They would not have endured that if it weren't true. Watergate embroiled 12 of the most powerful men in the world— and they couldn't keep a lie for three weeks. You're telling me 12 apostles could keep a lie for 40 years? Absolutely impossible."

Jesus is alive!

The death and burial of Jesus are recorded in John chapter 19. His resurrection does not occur until John chapter 20. However, John 11:25-26 records, ***"Jesus said to her, 'I am the resurrection and the life. Whoever believes in me, though he die, yet shall he live, and everyone who lives and believes in me shall never die. Do you believe this?'"***

Looking at these verses, what did Jesus call Himself?

_____

_____

Looking at the verses, what does that name mean?

_____

_____

_____

LESSON TEN JESUS ROSE AGAIN & THE ASCENSION

Mark 16:1-6 records what happened the morning of the resurrection, *"When the Sabbath was past, Mary Magdalene, Mary the mother of James, and Salome bought spices, so that they might go and anoint him. And very early on the first day of the week, when the sun had risen, they went to the tomb. And they were saying to one another, 'Who will roll away the stone for us from the entrance of the tomb?' And looking up, they saw that the stone had been rolled back—it was very large. And entering the tomb, they saw a young man sitting on the right side, dressed in a white robe, and they were alarmed. And he said to them, 'Do not be alarmed. You seek Jesus of Nazareth, who was crucified. He has risen; he is not here. See the place where they laid him.'"*

What was going to be the difficulty for the woman?

_____

_____

_____

Who speaks to the women?

_____

_____

_____

What is said to the women?

_____

_____

_____

Luke 24:5-7 says, *"And as they were frightened and bowed their faces to the ground, the men said to them, 'Why do you seek the living among the dead? He is not here, but has risen. Remember how he told you, while he was still in Galilee, that the Son of Man must be delivered into the hands of sinful men and be crucified and on the third day rise.'"*

LESSON TEN JESUS ROSE AGAIN & THE ASCENSION

What question is asked of the women?

_____

_____

_____

What did Jesus prophesy?

_____

_____

_____

1 Thessalonians 4:14 takes the resurrection to another level, *"For since we believe that Jesus died and rose again, even so, through Jesus, God will bring with him those who have fallen asleep."*

What does the resurrection mean to believers?

_____

_____

_____

Acts 1:3 gives an interesting fact, *"He presented himself alive to them after his suffering by many proofs, appearing to them during forty days and speaking about the kingdom of God."*

How long was Jesus on earth before He went back to Heaven?

_____

_____

_____

Paul writes in 1 Corinthians 15:3-8, *"For I delivered to you as of first importance what I also received: that Christ died for our sins in accordance with the Scriptures, that he was buried, that he was raised on the third day in accordance with the Scriptures,*

LESSON TEN JESUS ROSE AGAIN & THE ASCENSION

and that he appeared to Cephas, then to the twelve. Then he appeared to more than five hundred brothers at one time, most of whom are still alive, though some have fallen asleep. Then he appeared to James, then to all the apostles. Last of all, as to one untimely born, he appeared also to me."

How does Paul describe the Gospel?

_____

_____

_____

How many people did Jesus appear to after the resurrection?

_____

_____

_____

There were so many witnesses. Norman Geisler said, "If the Resurrection had not occurred, why would the apostle Paul give such a list of supposed eyewitnesses? He would immediately lose all credibility with his Corinthian readers by lying so blatantly."

John 20:24-29 records the story of Thomas after Jesus' resurrection. Verses 24-25 say, *"Now Thomas, one of the twelve, called the Twin, was not with them when Jesus came. So the other disciples told him, 'We have seen the Lord.' But he said to them, 'Unless I see in his hands the mark of the nails, and place my finger into the mark of the nails, and place my hand into his side, I will never believe.'"*

Why is Thomas sometimes called "Doubting Thomas?"

_____

_____

_____

228

LESSON TEN JESUS ROSE AGAIN & THE ASCENSION

Verses 26-29 continue the story, *"Eight days later, his disciples were inside again, and Thomas was with them. Although the doors were locked, Jesus came and stood among them and said, 'Peace be with you.' Then he said to Thomas, 'Put your finger here, and see my hands; and put out your hand, and place it in my side. Do not disbelieve, but believe.' Thomas answered him, 'My Lord and my God!' Jesus said to him, 'Have you believed because you have seen me? Blessed are those who have not seen and yet have believed.'"*

Was Jesus physically present or as a spirit?

_____

_____

_____

What does Thomas' response mean?

_____

_____

_____

Josh McDowell said, "No matter how devastating our struggles, disappointments, and troubles are, they are only temporary. No matter what happens to you, no matter the depth of tragedy or pain you face, no matter how death stalks you and your loved ones, the Resurrection promises you a future of immeasurable good."

How does this perspective comfort believers?

_____

_____

_____

Martin Luther added, "Our Lord has written the promise of resurrection, not in books alone, but in every leaf in springtime."

229

LESSON TEN JESUS ROSE AGAIN & THE ASCENSION

How is this a good visual?

_____

_____

_____

Acts 1:8-11 speaks of Jesus ascension back to Heaven, *"'But you will receive power when the Holy Spirit has come upon you, and you will be my witnesses in Jerusalem and in all Judea and Samaria, and to the end of the earth.' And when he had said these things, as they were looking on, he was lifted up, and a cloud took him out of their sight. And while they were gazing into heaven as he went, behold, two men stood by them in white robes, and said, 'Men of Galilee, why do you stand looking into heaven? This Jesus, who was taken up from you into heaven, will come in the same way as you saw him go into heaven.'"*

Who were the two men in white robes?

_____

_____

_____

What do the two men say?

_____

_____

_____

Where is Jesus now?

_____

_____

_____

LESSON TEN JESUS ROSE AGAIN & THE ASCENSION

What does it mean that He *"will come in the same way as you saw him go into heaven?"*

_____

_____

_____

"Few people seem to realize that the resurrection of Jesus is the cornerstone to a worldview that provides the perspective to all of life." Josh McDowell

LESSON TEN JESUS ROSE AGAIN & THE ASCENSION

1 THESSALONIANS 4:14

JESUS ROSE AGAIN & THE ASCENSION, DEVOTION 1
Ryan Story | *Student Pastor*

Jesus was there at creation. Jesus looked upon humanity after sin came into the world. Jesus watched as Abraham, Isaac, and Jacob lived out their covenants. Jesus watched as Moses lead the Israelites out of Egypt. Jesus watched as David defeated Goliath. Jesus watched as Solomon made Israel the strongest nation in the world. Jesus watched as Babylon and Assyria sacked Judah and Israel. Jesus watched as the remnant came back to rebuild their kingdom. Jesus watched all those moments in history happen until the day He came to be born. Jesus died on the cross. Jesus fulfilled God's will. Jesus paid the price that we could not pay ourselves. All of that is worthy of what an amazing God has done for us, but the crown jewel of all of the acts of Jesus is that He rose again.

1 Thessalonians 4:14 says, ***"For since we believe that Jesus died and rose again."*** It is a factual statement. It is as factual to say that Jesus rose from the dead as it is to say that water is wet. There has never been any historical document that has ever disproved the fact that Jesus rose from the grave. There has never been a movement against Christ that has ever buried, derailed, or slowed down the amazing truth that Jesus rose again. There has never been a king, dictator, ideology, or philosophy that has been able to rule over the fact that Jesus rose from the grave. The truest statement that we can say is that Jesus did, in fact, die and He did, in fact, rise from the grave.

We live in a society that only likes to reason in the physical realm. We no longer believe history as fact but as a narrative to those who

JESUS ROSE AGAIN & THE ASCENSION DEVOTION 1

win. We live in a world where on July 21, 1969, everyone woke up and everyone was in awe of the fact that on the previous day man just landed on the moon. Fast-forward thirty years and people now believe that it was a hoax. We live in a world where despite the fact there has never been any document that disproved Jesus' resurrection, 2000 years after this amazing event people believe it was just a story for the weak-minded. Every Christian should know and preach every day that "He has risen!"

We as Christ followers must make sure that the resurrection is at the cornerstone of our relationship. We are meant to live our lives in constant identification to the fact that our Savior rose again. The significance of the resurrection from death to life is shown in our lives of dying to our former self and rising to newness of life. Take a moment today and figure out how you show the world that you have the power of the resurrection living inside of you.

MARK 16:1-6

JESUS ROSE AGAIN & THE ASCENSION, DEVOTION 2
James Clouse | *Student Pastor*

Have you ever had a time where you went to a store looking to find something, and you did not find it? Have you searched for that one ingredient you needed for the one recipe for which you were responsible? In Georgia, we lived in a college town. Most of the time living in a college town was great. It was awesome seeing all the young people walking around, the opportunities for ministry were limitless, the excitement in the city was great (most of the time). The time where it was not so great was the move-in weekend. The grocery store shelves were empty during this time. You could not walk into the grocery store and get your whole list of things you needed; it was next to impossible. But if I went to the grocery store in the town over I could get what I needed. Before, I was just looking in the wrong place.

In Mark, we read a story of Mary Magdalene and some other women going to the tomb of Jesus. They get there to see that the stone had been removed from in front of the tomb. Mark 16:1-6 says,

"When the Sabbath was past, Mary Magdalene, Mary the mother of James, and Salome bought spices, so that they might go and anoint him. And very early on the first day of the week, when the sun had risen, they went to the tomb. And they were saying to one another, 'Who will roll away the stone for us from the entrance of the tomb?' And looking up, they saw that the stone had been rolled back—it was very large. And entering the tomb, they saw a young man sitting on the right side, dressed in a white robe, and they were alarmed. And he said to them, 'Do

JESUS ROSE AGAIN & THE ASCENSION DEVOTION 2

not be alarmed. You seek Jesus of Nazareth, who was crucified. He has risen; he is not here. See the place where they laid him.'"

Jesus has risen! Mary and the other women had not known that this had happened. They came to the tomb expecting to see Jesus. However, when they got there, the body was gone. I love the exact words the angel uses when he says, *"He has risen; He is not here."* He is telling them that they are looking in the wrong place for Jesus. He is no longer in the grave but has risen from the grave.

People of our world often look for salvation in the wrong places. They look for salvation in drugs, sex, money, success, or alcohol. Let me tell you, if you are looking for salvation in those things then you are looking in the wrong place. There is only one place you can find salvation, and that is in the name of Christ Jesus, who has risen from the grave for you and me.

LUKE 24:5-7

JESUS ROSE AGAIN & THE ASCENSION, DEVOTION 3
Jayson Combs | *Family Pastor*

Is it all a scam? Did Jesus die and rise from the dead? This question and its implications are vital for us to consider as believers. For without a literal raising from the dead, all of Christianity is in vain. As Paul states in one of his letters to the early church, our faith is "useless" if Jesus did not rise.

There are many skeptics. Some will say it was an illusion organized by His followers. Others say Jesus did not die on the cross, and therefore He never had to rise from the dead (although Mark chapter 15 tells us Pilate carefully made sure He was dead). Some critics say that Jesus did die, but the disciples kidnapped His body (even though Matthew chapter 27 tells us the tomb was guarded by Roman Soldiers). Here are a couple of points I think are very helpful when considering Christ's resurrection.

First, take time to read Luke chapter 24. You will read about a few ladies traveling to Jesus' grave on the first day of the week to finish preparing His body for burial. When the women arrive at the tomb, they find the stone rolled away and the body of Jesus gone. Instead of being excited, they were perplexed and afraid. Immediately, the women left to tell the disciples what they had found. But rather than believing Jesus rose from the dead (as Jesus had claimed He would), the disciples themselves believed the women to be lying. It was not until later when Jesus appeared to the disciples in the Upper Room that they finally believed.

Luke 24:10-11 says, ***"Now it was Mary Magdalene and Joanna and Mary the mother of James and the other women with them***

JESUS ROSE AGAIN & THE ASCENSION DEVOTION 3

who told these things to the apostles, but these words seemed to them an idle tale, and they did not believe them."

Next, the Bible teaches that Jesus spent 40 days on Earth after His resurrection. Acts chapter 1 gives an account of the final interaction between Jesus and His disciples before He ascends to Heaven. Jesus gives the disciples instructions on how to live after He is gone. After the ascension, Scripture reveals the determination and passion of the disciples to live out the call given by Jesus. But the disciples were met with much opposition. In Acts 12:1-3, we read, *"Herod the king laid violent hands on some who belonged to the church. He killed James the brother of John with the sword, and when he saw that it pleased the Jews, he proceeded to arrest Peter also."* In this passage, we learn that James, the brother of John (the disciple) was killed for his belief in Christ. Other accounts reveal many were beaten and killed because of their faith in Christ and the resurrection.

Therefore, knowing the disciples were under severe persecution and even martyred for their faith in Christ, there is another question I must ask myself regarding the disciples and the resurrection of Jesus, "Why would the disciples be willing to die for their faith in Jesus if it was just a hoax and He did not really rise from the dead?" In other words, why would the disciples put their lives on the line for something they knew to be a lie? It does not make sense.

Rather, the accounts of the disciples provide compelling evidence that Jesus did rise from the grave, appeared to the disciples, and inspired the disciples to give their lives so that many would come to know Jesus as Messiah.

Personally, you must also consider the questions, "Did Jesus rise?" and "Why would the disciples give their lives for the Christ?" If you

JESUS ROSE AGAIN & THE ASCENSION DEVOTION 3

believe He rose from the dead, then Jesus is God; and if He is God, He deserves all of our worship and praise. How will you live out your life to glorify and praise Him as our resurrected Messiah?

JESUS ROSE AGAIN & THE ASCENSION DEVOTION 3

JOHN 20:24-29

JESUS ROSE AGAIN & THE ASCENSION, DEVOTION 4
Caleb Combs | *Gathering Pastor*

I am an avid sports fan, Okay, sometimes in an unhealthy way, I will watch or play anything. I recently had the opportunity to travel to Israel for a Holy Land experience. One night at the hotel, I found myself watching a game called snooker. It is a version of billiards with some very interesting rules. I googled the rules so I could follow along in the match. Yes, I am that guy. I love the art of competition and sport; it is enthralling. On November 20, 1982, the world experienced one of the greatest plays in the history of sports. It was a college football game between the California Bears and Stanford Cardinals. They were and are still rivals, with each matchup being highly anticipated. The game went back and forth with both teams holding leads in the game. John Elway, the quarterback for Stanford, found himself down two points late in the fourth quarter. He was able to lead his team down the field for a field goal with four seconds left to take the lead and seemingly capture the most important win. The team celebrated because they had just taken down their rival. They poured the Gatorade jug over the head coach and celebrated this incredible victory. However, by rule, there were four seconds left on the clock, and they must kick the ball off to the other team. The announcer, Joe Starkey said, "Only a miracle can save the Bears now!" If you know the situation, you know what happened next. The term "The Play" was coined because the Cal Bears would take the kickoff back for a touchdown. It is one of the craziest plays you will ever see (trust me, if you have not seen it go check it out on YouTube) that included five laterals. The Stanford players, coaches, and even the band came on the field thinking they had won. The California Bears walked away victorious against their greatest rival in one of the biggest turn of events in sports' history.

JESUS ROSE AGAIN & THE ASCENSION DEVOTION 4

This story reminds me of another turn of events in the history of the world, and Cal's win does not come close to touching it in the level of importance. I am referencing the resurrection and victory of our Savior Jesus Christ. After Jesus died on the cross and paid the debt we owed with His own life; He was put into a tomb. It was a tomb where everyone thought He would stay; His followers even came to put oils and spices on His body. There was no hope; death had won. Jesus' greatest rival, Satan, began to celebrate his victory. I can just imagine, Satan and his followers celebrating because they had finally defeated Jesus. He was dead, and the story was over. Oh wait, the game was not over. The tomb could not hold Jesus. Death had no victory because Jesus Christ conquered Death, Hell, and the Grave and walked out victorious. When no one else thought there was hope, and the "announcers" said only a miracle can save Him now, that in fact was exactly what happened. It was the greatest comeback in the history of the world, and one I am thankful for every minute of every day.

I mentioned that Jesus' followers had even given up on Him. It is just like the game between Stanford and Cal. When Stanford seemingly captured the victory in the closing seconds, most fans of Cal began to head home. They "knew" the game was over and there was no hope. The same happened to Jesus' followers. Many went home dejected and disappointed knowing they had lost. In the days following Jesus' victory, He would appear to His followers and show them His victory; they were amazed and astonished. One follower, named Thomas was still in disbelief. He saw with his own eyes Satan's victory and headed home.

In John 20:24-29 we pick up in the story. *"Now Thomas, one of the twelve, called the Twin, was not with them when Jesus came. So the other disciples told him, "We have seen the Lord.' But he said to them, 'Unless I see in his hands the mark of the*

JESUS ROSE AGAIN & THE ASCENSION DEVOTION 4

nails, and place my finger into the mark of the nails, and place my hand into his side, I will never believe.' Eight days later, his disciples were inside again, and Thomas was with them. Although the doors were locked, Jesus came and stood among them and said, 'Peace be with you.' Then he said to Thomas, 'Put your finger here, and see my hands; and put out your hand, and place it in my side. Do not disbelieve, but believe.' Thomas answered him, 'My Lord and my God!' Jesus said to him, 'Have you believed because you have seen me? Blessed are those who have not seen and yet have believed.'" Thomas needed to see the victory with His own eyes, and Jesus showed up. The victory Jesus earned is given to us. So may you today truly understand the greatest victory in the history of the world, Jesus Christ!

JESUS ROSE AGAIN & THE ASCENSION DEVOTION 4

1 CORINTHIANS 15:3-8

JESUS ROSE AGAIN & THE ASCENSION, DEVOTION 5
Chuck Lindsey | *Reach Pastor*

"For I delivered to you first of all that which I also received: that Christ died for our sins according to the Scriptures, and that He was buried, and that He rose again the third day according to the Scriptures, and that He was seen by Cephas, then by the twelve. After that He was seen by over five hundred brethren at once, of whom the greater part remain to the present, but some have fallen asleep. After that He was seen by James, then by all the apostles. Then last of all He was seen by me also, as by one born out of due time." 1 Corinthians 15:3-8 (NKJV)

What if Jesus had never risen from the dead? What I mean is, what if He had come, taught us all that He taught us, showed us all He showed us, even died on the cross, was buried in the tomb, but that was it? What if that was where the story ended? What I am asking is, what if Jesus had not risen from the dead? Would it change anything? Could we just go on as we always have? Does anything change?

We do not need to guess about this. First Corinthians chapter 15, tells us exactly what it would mean if Jesus did not rise from the dead. It would have been the end of Christianity. It is not an exaggeration to say that Christianity would have been over before it even began! Jesus would have faded into the background of history as any other good man or teacher, and we would not be having this conversation. In short, it would mean that we are not saved, that our sins are not forgiven, and that we have no hope at all!

JESUS ROSE AGAIN & THE ASCENSION DEVOTION 5

The denial of the resurrection is nothing new. Following the resurrection, many tried to explain it away or dismiss it altogether. Some suggested that Jesus never actually even died, that He revived (and somehow in His weakened state rolled back a 2-ton stone by Himself and all of His disciples died knowing He was lying). Some suggested that He died, but never actually rose from the dead at all, that the disciples came in the night and stole His body (overpowering the Roman guards and again, each of them dying knowing that the whole thing was a farce). One of the heresies (false doctrine) that was being spread by false teachers in the days of the early church was the idea that Jesus Christ did not rise from the dead physically. These heretics taught that when Christ rose from the dead, He only did so "spiritually." Most of them also said that He only came "spiritually" teaching that He left no footprints when He walked. The apostle's (especially Paul) continually fought against these false teachers and their false doctrine.

In 1 Corinthians chapter 15, Paul dealt with the bodily resurrection of Christ. He said that Jesus Christ not only died and was buried (you can not bury a spirit!) but He also rose from the dead the third day. He said this was all according to the promise of the Scriptures. He does not stop there. What he says next is so important. He says Jesus was seen alive by Peter (Cephas), then by the 12 disciples, and then by over 500 others at one time. Now here is the kicker, Paul says, "They are all still alive! Ask them what they saw! They will tell you." He goes on and says, "He was seen by His brother James, then by all of the apostles and then, I saw Him myself."

Now, it is certainly possible to get a few people to go in together on a lie. But how many are willing to die for what they know is a lie? Christians were being persecuted and killed for saying that Christ was alive. How many would be willing to die knowing it was all a lie? Even if over 500 people were in on the lie, how many of them

JESUS ROSE AGAIN & THE ASCENSION DEVOTION 5

would have maintained that lie while being persecuted, tortured, and killed for that lie? The answer is very few if any. If it were a lie, it would have eventually been exposed as such and Christianity, and indeed Christ, would have faded into the background of history amid scandal as so many others have.

But we do not have that. We have countless eyewitness Christians with their dying breath proclaiming that He is risen! They are convinced they saw Him alive. They had touched Him. They watched Him as He both rose from the dead and ascended 40 days later into Heaven before their eyes.

JESUS ROSE AGAIN & THE ASCENSION DEVOTION 5

ACTS 1:3

JESUS ROSE AGAIN & THE ASCENSION, DEVOTION 6
Joshua Combs | *Lead Pastor*

"He presented himself alive to them after His suffering by many proofs, appearing to them during forty days and speaking about the kingdom of God." Acts 1:3

As the lives of many historically important military, political, social, and religious leaders come to an end, either by age or in some cases by assassination or other tragedies, society begins to memorialize them, honor them through the building of monuments or museums, or other means of transforming a cultural figure into an icon. Martin Luther King Jr. and both John and Bobby Kennedy were each assassinated at what appeared to be the prime of their lives. Entertainers who have died due to a drug overdose, plane crashes, or car accidents instantly have their last movie or album celebrated as their final work. Military figures who die in battle or win wars have been remembered with statues that can be found all around the world. Even today as I write this, I received the news that Dr. Billy Graham has gone to Heaven at the age of 99. No evangelist or preacher in modern time has had the global impact of Graham. His legacy will live on for decades to come. For many, Jesus of Nazareth falls within this same scope, relegated to simply a brilliant teacher, political figure, and founder of a global religious movement. But one single event sets Jesus apart from everyone else: The Resurrection.

Jesus did not stay dead. He rose again after being dead and buried for three days. This single, historical event creates the lens through which we view every other facet of Jesus' life and ministry. Years

JESUS ROSE AGAIN & THE ASCENSION DEVOTION 6

after Jesus' resurrection, the Apostle Paul writes, *"He appeared to more than five hundred brothers at one time, most of whom are still alive, though some have fallen asleep"* (1 Corinthians 15:6). Jesus' resurrection was attested by 500 people who saw Jesus, not at separate, individual times, but at once. Jesus rose again and to demonstrate the validity of this, He gave us *"many proofs"* (Acts 1:3). After suffering the unspeakable wrath of the cross, dying, and rising again, He would eat with the disciples, talk with friends, travel on the road to Emmaus, teach, allow His wounds to be examined by Thomas, and many more proofs.

The idea of Jesus' bodily resurrection is a fact attested to by hundreds of witnesses and further proved by the fact that many of them would themselves face death by martyrdom for believing, preaching, and professing this reality. The Scripture is clear, *"...in fact Christ has been raised from the dead"* (1 Corinthians 15:20).

JESUS ROSE AGAIN & THE ASCENSION DEVOTION 6

11

THE RETURN OF CHRIST

**DR. RANDY T. JOHNSON,
GROWTH PASTOR**

LESSON ELEVEN THE RETURN OF CHRIST

like famous movie lines. In studying the return of Christ one key scenario comes to mind. In his 1984 movie, *"Terminator,"* Arnold Schwarzenegger boldly proclaims, "I'll be back." He immediately returned to quite the scene. He kept his word. I view Jesus, with more power than Arnold could ever imagine, saying with words of comfort, but warning, "I will be back!" Jesus is coming back. He will keep His word.

Maybe you are more of a fan of history and remember General Douglas MacArthur. During World War II, he promised the people of the Philippines, "I Shall Return." He did keep his word.

Acts 1 records Jesus leaving for Heaven. Right after He ascends, an angel says, ***"Men of Galilee, why do you stand looking into heaven? This Jesus, who was taken up from you into heaven, will come in the same way as you saw him go into heaven"*** (verse 11). As soon as He leaves, we are reminded that He will return.

How will the Lord return?

_____

_____

_____

"Both the Old and New Testaments are filled with promises of the Second Coming of Christ. There are 1,845 references to it in the Old Testament, and a total of seventeen Old Testament books give it prominence. Of the 260 chapters in the entire New Testament, there are 318 references to the Second Coming, or one out of 30 verses. Twenty-three of the 27 New Testament books refer to this great event. The four missing books include three which are single-chapter letters written to individual persons on a particular subject, and the fourth is Galatians which does imply Christ's coming again. For every prophecy on the First Coming of Christ, there are 8 on Christ's Second Coming." Paul Lee Tan

LESSON ELEVEN THE RETURN OF CHRIST

What points stand out most in this quote?

_____

_____

_____

Does this quote surprise you? Why or why not?

_____

_____

_____

1 Thessalonians 4:13-18 says, *"But we do not want you to be uninformed, brothers, about those who are asleep, that you may not grieve as others do who have no hope. For since we believe that Jesus died and rose again, even so, through Jesus, God will bring with him those who have fallen asleep. For this we declare to you by a word from the Lord, that we who are alive, who are left until the coming of the Lord, will not precede those who have fallen asleep. For the Lord himself will descend from heaven with a cry of command, with the voice of an archangel, and with the sound of the trumpet of God. And the dead in Christ will rise first. Then we who are alive, who are left, will be caught up together with them in the clouds to meet the Lord in the air, and so we will always be with the Lord. Therefore encourage one another with these words."*

What does *"grieve as others do who have no hope"* mean?

_____

_____

_____

LESSON ELEVEN THE RETURN OF CHRIST

What is necessary for one to have hope?

_____

_____

_____

Describe what is pictured here.

_____

_____

_____

What is the goal of these words?

_____

_____

_____

The parables of Jesus Christ often refer to His return. Look up each parable, write down what the parable is, and mention how it relates to the topic.

Matthew 24:44-51: _____

_____

_____

Matthew 25:1-13: _____

_____

_____

Matthew 25:14-30: _____

_____

_____

Luke 12:35-38: _____

_____

_____

LESSON ELEVEN THE RETURN OF CHRIST

Luke 12:39-40: _____

_____

_____

Luke 21:25-36: _____

_____

_____

In 2 Peter 3:10-12 it says, *"But the day of the Lord will come like a thief, and then the heavens will pass away with a roar, and the heavenly bodies will be burned up and dissolved, and the earth and the works that are done on it will be exposed. Since all these things are thus to be dissolved, what sort of people ought you to be in lives of holiness and godliness, waiting for and hastening the coming of the day of God, because of which the heavens will be set on fire and dissolved, and the heavenly bodies will melt as they burn!"*

Will the Lord's return be well announced or a surprise?

_____

_____

_____

Knowing that the Lord could return at any time, how are we told to live?

_____

_____

_____

"When He returns is not as important as the fact that we are ready for Him when He does return." A.W. Tozer

256

LESSON ELEVEN THE RETURN OF CHRIST

What does this quote mean?

_____

_____

_____

The last two verses of the Bible (Revelation 22:20-21) say, *"He who testifies to these things says, 'Surely I am coming soon.' Amen. Come, Lord Jesus! The grace of the Lord Jesus be with all. Amen."*

What is the very last message of the Bible?

_____

_____

_____

"Precisely because we cannot predict the moment, we must be ready at all moments." C.S. Lewis

Jesus will return. He will be back!

LESSON ELEVEN THE RETURN OF CHRIST

MATTHEW 24:44-45

THE RETURN OF CHRIST, DEVOTION 1
Ryan Story | *Student Pastor*

Working with high school students, I have developed a few questions I like using each year. One of my favorite questions to ask is: "If God came to you and asked, 'You have a choice. Choice one, I will come back right now, and the rapture will happen. Or choice two, I will wait exactly one year. What do you choose?'" I enjoy watching students struggle with the implications of this question. Almost every time the majority of students choose choice two. It is not that they do not want to be with Jesus in Heaven, they just always look at their lives and realize that they are not ready. They feel they need to evangelize to loved ones. They feel they need to take another look at their walk with Jesus and make sure they are not on the rough end of Matthew 7:21. As the conversation is concluding, I always encourage every student that their walk with God should show that they are ready for His return at any time.

Matthew 24:44 says, ***"Therefore you also must be ready, for the Son of Man is coming at an hour you do not expect."*** One of the key fundamental facts about our God is that He is, in fact, coming back. Jesus came to this Earth, loved and healed people, gave up His life on a Roman cross in order that we might be made righteous in God's sight, and returned to the right hand of the Father. He did all of that close to two thousand years ago. There is one major event that has yet to happen, Christ's return for His bride. The hardest part of the whole return thing is He never left an exact time. Every Bible verse that has to do with His return is shrouded in mystery. The clear and somewhat frustrating reality is that we know He is coming but He never gave us a time.

THE RETURN OF CHRIST DEVOTION 1

Sadly, most of us do not live our lives in a way that shows we are eagerly awaiting our King's return. At times we may look down at younger Christians for answering choice two in that hypothetical question. We need to take a moment and be honest with ourselves, are we ready for Jesus to come back? It is hard to live out our walk with Jesus with such jubilant excitement every day of our lives. It is easy to have a relationship with God that seems to be built on doing. Luckily for us, Jesus already did everything for us. Our relationship with God should never be based on us doing. He already did; He arose and will return.

Matthew chapter 24 offers some amazing advice. Matthew 24:45 says, *"Who then is the faithful and wise servant."* So how do we live a life that is always focused on His return? We as Christians must be faithful and wise in all our actions. We must be faithful to glorify Him with all of the time, and in front of all the people we encounter. We must be wise to figure out what are the important things we must focus on and what are the urgent things that take us away from the important things. But remember, He is coming back. Are you ready?

LUKE 12:35-38

THE RETURN OF CHRIST, DEVOTION 2
Tommy Youngquist | *Children's Pastor*

I am about to be way too honest with you, but there are times in my life where I will think about the second coming of Jesus, and the thought will run through my head, "Not Yet!" I mean, there are so many things I want to experience in this life. My wife and I just had our first child, and we want to see her grow up. I want to have more children. I want to see the world. I want to experience being a grandfather. "There are so many things I want to happen before my life is over," I will think to myself. But then I check myself, and I have to realize that when Jesus comes back, true life begins! It will be a life that is so much better than the one I have here. Imagine eternal life in a world that is perfect.

The Bible says in Luke 12:35-38, *"Stay dressed for action and keep your lamps burning, and be like men who are waiting for their master to come home from the wedding feast, so that they may open the door to him at once when he comes and knocks. Blessed are those servants whom the master finds awake when he comes. Truly, I say to you, he will dress himself for service and have them recline at table, and he will come and serve them. If he comes in the second watch, or in the third, and finds them awake, blessed are those servants!"*

We are not only supposed to be ready for the return of Christ, but we are supposed to be anticipating it! *"Stay dressed for action,"* Luke says. Something is coming, and you need to be ready for it. Be prepared. You should be thriving with anticipation because it could happen at any second!

THE RETURN OF CHRIST DEVOTION 2

When my focus shifts from "Not Yet" to "Get ready for Awesome," my priorities change during my daily routine. Instead of focusing on earning money to do all of the things I think I want to do, I focus on the only thing I can take with me to that "Awesome." Human souls are on balance. I will spend more time with Ashley and Heidi. I will spend more time with the RiverKids. When I am forced to decide between earthly or eternal, I am more apt to choose eternally. Part of preparing for the second coming of Christ is doing everything humanly possible to get as many other people ready as you can. Are you doing that? Are you going to be the blessed servant that is awake when Jesus comes back? Or is your mindset "Not yet?"

2 PETER 3:10-18

THE RETURN OF CHRIST, DEVOTION 3
Jayson Combs | *Family Pastor*

My 7-year old son and I have a little game we like to play. The game could be called "I will hide from you and at the perfect moment, I will jump out to make you terrified." It is a wonderful game, and if I do say so myself, I have gotten to be pretty good at our little game. When I arrive home, I strategically look through the mirrors in our home, knowing where my son likes to hide. Instead of him scaring me, I usually scare him. Again, it is a wonderful game!

In 1 Thessalonians 5:2 (NIV), Paul gives us a glimpse into the return of Christ. He says in verse 10, *"The day of the Lord will come like a thief in the night."* Peter then provides more details of Jesus' coming and follows up in with a challenge for the church.

"Therefore, beloved, since you are waiting for these, be diligent to be found by him without spot or blemish, and at peace" (2 Peter 3:14).

Peter's challenge is clear. Because we know the return of Christ is coming, we ought to live holy and godly lives. He urges those of us in the church to reflect on what kind of person we are going to be. It is interesting to consider the word "diligent," used by Peter in the passage above. As Warren Wiersbe suggests, "we are to have an 'expectant attitude' that will make a difference in our conduct." Paul also encourages Titus, in Titus 2:13 to wait *"for our blessed hope, the appearing of the glory of our great God and Savior Jesus Christ."* If we lose sight of that blessed hope, we are in grave danger of losing our walk with Him.

THE RETURN OF CHRIST DEVOTION 3

In Mark chapter 13, Jesus speaks specifically about his return (I encourage you to take time to read the entire chapter). Jesus uses the phrase *"guard yourself"* multiple times. The KJV translates it as *"take heed."* Over and over, Jesus warns the people to take heed (verses 5, 9, 23, and 33). Verse 33 specifically says, *"Be on guard, keep awake. For you do not know when the time will come."* In other words, be alert and be ready. This is not because we know the specific day and the specific time, but because we have a specific call on our lives as followers of Christ. This call is to live diligently, intentionally, holy, and godly every minute of every day. We are to be "making every effort to be found spotless, blameless and at peace with him."

I remember coming home one day, forgetting about the little game I played with my son. He slipped behind a wall without me knowing. As I walked around the corner, he jumped out and scared me really good. He was so thrilled that he finally got his dad. I hope that we do not become so focused on the things of this world that we forget about the Lord's return.

REVELATION 22:20-21

THE RETURN OF CHRIST, DEVOTION 4
Caleb Combs | *Gathering Pastor*

Growing up, our youth group went to Hiawatha Youth Camp each summer. I have some incredible memories and friends I keep in touch with to this day made from the weeks on Piot Lake in the beautiful Upper Peninsula of Michigan. One memory I have is of a girl singing a song. Her name was Angela Carpenter, and she sang the most impactful song I had ever heard in my life. The song was by Crystal Lewis and its called, *"People get ready... Jesus is Comin."* I remember sitting in the auditorium as a thirteen-year-old boy thinking to myself about this song. I attached the lyrics and encourage you to check it out on YouTube, iTunes, or some other media source.

Lord, I'm ready now
I'm waiting for Your triumphant return
You're coming so soon
This world has nothing for me
I find my peace and joy solely in You
Only in You
I want the world to see that
You're alive and living well in me
Let me be a part of the harvest
For the days are few
He's coming soon

People get ready Jesus is coming
Soon we'll be going home
People get ready Jesus is coming
To take from the world His own

THE RETURN OF CHRIST DEVOTION 4

There will be a day
When we will be divided right and left
For those who know Him
And those who do not know
Those who know Him well
Will meet Him in the air
Hallelujah
God is with us
Those who do not know
They will hear "Depart, I knew you not."
For my friends you see
There will be a day when we'll be counted
So know Him well, know Him well

People get ready Jesus is coming
Soon we'll be going home
People get ready Jesus is coming
To take from the world His own

After hearing her sing this song, I can still recall exactly how I felt. The song was dynamic and beautiful, even moving some to tears, but in me, it created a different emotion. It created fear. I felt scared for the return of Christ. The very last words in the Bible, found in Revelation 22: 20-21, tell us that *"He who testifies to these things says, 'Surely I am coming soon.' Amen. Come, Lord Jesus! The grace of the Lord Jesus be with all. Amen"* A great message of the return of a Savior should bring comfort and joy, but I did not feel that. I knew Jesus was my Lord and Savior and had committed my life to Him, yet something about His return created fear and anxiety in me. Looking back at this memory, I can now understand why I felt that way (13-year-old boys cannot explain anything!). 2 Peter 3:14 is a great explanation for me. *"Therefore, beloved, since you are waiting for these, be diligent to be found by Him without spot*

THE RETURN OF CHRIST DEVOTION 4

or blemish, and at peace." That word *"diligent"* is so convicting because it requires action on my part. It is not required for salvation or entrance into Heaven, but it is a charge to us as believers. Revelation is clear - He is coming back. No man knows the day or the hour for the return of Christ, but we are given clear direction for when He returns - be busy doing His work. As a 13-year-old, I was not busy in the work of Jesus Christ. I liked to live life according to my desires and do my things, and that continued into my twenties. But this verse is an attention grabber. Christ could return tomorrow, and how will He find me? How will He find you?

The words of the song are clear, *"people get ready, Jesus is coming."* To the unbeliever, I beg you to get ready by giving your life to Christ. No one is guaranteed tomorrow! To the believer, are you diligently at work for Christ? That does not mean you have to quit your job and move to a foreign country and start preaching (if you are called to this, then do it!). You are called to shine the light of Christ in your workplace, your family, and all those around you. We as followers of Christ have an incredible opportunity to point people to Jesus. There is no need for anxiety or fear when it comes to Christ's return. Take it from someone who has conquered this feeling. Now, I just want to be found *"diligent!"* May we live our lives today like He will return tomorrow, knowing that there are millions around the world and across the street that need to hear about Jesus!

THE RETURN OF CHRIST DEVOTION 4

1 THESSALONIANS 4:13-18

THE RETURN OF CHRIST, DEVOTION 5
Chuck Lindsey | *Reach Pastor*

"But I do not want you to be ignorant, brethren, concerning those who have fallen asleep, lest you sorrow as others who have no hope. For if we believe that Jesus died and rose again, even so God will bring with Him those who sleep in Jesus. For this we say to you by the word of the Lord, that we who are alive and remain until the coming of the Lord will by no means precede those who are asleep. For the Lord Himself will descend from heaven with a shout, with the voice of an archangel, and with the trumpet of God. And the dead in Christ will rise first. Then we who are alive and remain shall be caught up together with them in the clouds to meet the Lord in the air. And thus we shall always be with the Lord. Therefore comfort one another with these words."
1 Thessalonians 4:13-18 (NKJV)

"When will Christ return?" is a question I have been asked numerous times through the years, and it is a question that has sparked much debate throughout the church age. But we are going to settle it right here and right now. Are you ready? No, I am asking you, "Are you ready?" That is the answer; be ready! The answer to "when is Jesus coming back?" is to be ready for Him to come back at any time.

Jesus said, *"Watch, therefore, for you know neither the day nor the hour in which the Son of Man is coming"* Matthew 25:13 (NKJV).

He also said, *"Therefore you also be ready, for the Son of Man is coming at an hour you do not expect"* Matthew 24:44 (NKJV).

THE RETURN OF CHRIST DEVOTION 5

Pre-trib, mid-trib, post-trib, Mc-Rib (lol), are all (except for that last one) ways of talking about when exactly Christ will come. The "pre-trib" view (which also happens to be the right view, haha) says that Jesus Christ will appear before the tribulation period (described in detail in Revelation chapters 6-19) to take all believers out of the world and into Heaven to be with Him forever. The "mid-trib" view says that Jesus will appear during the tribulation, taking all believers out of the world and into Heaven before the wrath of God being poured out on the whole world during the last 3 1/2 years of the 7-year tribulation period. The "post-trib" view says that there is no taking of believers to Heaven, but that Christ will come back to Earth at the end of the tribulation period and rule and reign forever.

Now, we can debate these views, we can argue our points, but the truth is, no one knows when He will come. That is what He said. He said He would come at an hour we do not expect Him. But hear this, "He is coming." We can be sure about that.

In 1 Thessalonians 4:13 we have an interesting situation. It seems that the Thessalonian believers were very troubled concerning the return of Christ. It is clear from this passage and many others that the early Christians lived their lives expecting that Jesus would return at any moment. They understood that when He returned, they would be "changed." They would immediately put on a "new heavenly body" if you will, to enter Heaven. But then the question, what about their loved ones who died long ago? What would happen to them? Will they be "changed" or are they just tough out of luck? Paul's words to them assure them that Christ has no problem raising their deceased ("sleeping") loved ones at His coming. We will all be together when He comes. It was meant to comfort them, and it did.

There are two things we must understand and agree on regardless of where you land on eschatological (end times) debates. First,

Christ is coming. Do not forget that or lose sight of it. Second, He can come at any moment. It will be at an hour we do not expect.

These were the realities that the early Christians understood. Day by day they looked for His coming. The Bible tells us that this is right and good for us as His people. 1 John 3:3 (NKJV) says, *"Everyone who has this hope in Him purifies himself, just as He is pure."* Jesus said, *"Surely I am coming quickly."* and so we say with Apostle John *"Even so, come Lord Jesus!"* Revelation 22:20 (NKJV).

THE RETURN OF CHRIST DEVOTION 5

MATTHEW 25:13

THE RETURN OF CHRIST, DEVOTION 6
Joshua Combs | *Lead Pastor*

"Watch therefore, for you know neither the day nor the hour."** Matthew 25:13

Jesus is coming back. That simple phrase may thrill your heart or go right in one ear and out the other. Hearing that Jesus is returning may be old news to you, or it may incite apocalyptic prepping. Regardless of your specific view on end times, current cultural trends, astrological interpretations, historical patterns, the stock market, or whichever particular way you receive the news of Christ's imminent return, the fact remains, Jesus is coming back to earth.

Throughout Jesus' ministry, He often spoke of His impending death on the cross. The disciples were so taken back by this thought, that Peter even rebuked Jesus for implying such (in Peter's view) nonsense (Matthew 16:22-23). Jesus also talked at length of His return as Holy Judge.

Many parables taught an incredibly important principle for believers throughout all ages. We must live every day ready and eagerly prepared for the arrival of Jesus Christ. In Matthew chapters 24 and 25, we read a sermon, or more appropriately, a conversation that Jesus had with His disciples on the Mount of Olives. Just to the east of the temple, Jesus sat on a hillside that provides, even to this day, a beautiful, panoramic view of the city of Jerusalem and, more specifically, the temple mount. He began to speak to them about the impending destruction of the temple (70 AD) and His return. Keep in mind that He had yet to die, be buried, or rise from the dead,

THE RETURN OF CHRIST DEVOTION 6

so this conversation would have been difficult to understand. But Jesus gave the disciples and us two main tasks to be doing while the master is away. Simply put, Jesus tells us to watch and work.

We must be watching for His return (Matthew 25:13). We cannot become so enamored with this world that we are not setting our hope in the kingdom yet to come. We must not just be watching, but working, diligently for the Master. He has entrusted to each of us His treasures that we must daily be using to further the Lord's interests. Watch and work - that is our call while we wait for the return of the Lord.

THE RETURN OF CHRIST DEVOTION 6

12

HELL & HEAVEN

**DR. RANDY T. JOHNSON,
GROWTH PASTOR**

LESSON TWELVE HELL & HEAVEN

Hell and Heaven are real, actual places of eternity. A description is probably not necessary as people regularly use the words. The word "Hell" is spoken by people who do not even believe in God: hotter than Hell, it will be a cold day in Hell, come Hell or high water, not a chance in Hell, it hurts like Hell, give them Hell, and go to Hell! If they want to give the extreme opposite analogy, they might say: A marriage made in Heaven, good Heavens, in Hog Heaven, Heaven help us, Heaven on earth, Heaven sent, it is heavenly, or even some paradise references. Hell is the epitome of negative, horrible, abominable, grotesque, appalling, and awful, while Heaven is portrayed as glorious, delightful, divine, wonderful, paradisiacal, perfect, and blissful.

What other phrases have you heard for Hell?

_____

_____

_____

What other phrases have you heard for Heaven?

_____

_____

_____

Everyone will end up in either place forever.

John 3:16 is one of the most famous verses in the Bible. This verse refers to both places, *"For God so loved the world, that he gave his only Son, that whoever believes in him should not perish but have eternal life."*

How are both places described here?

_____

_____

_____

LESSON TWELVE HELL & HEAVEN

What determines each person's destination?

_____

_____

_____

Romans 6:23 says, *"For the wages of sin is death, but the free gift of God is eternal life in Christ Jesus our Lord."*

Where does one find eternal life?

_____

_____

_____

Romans 2:6-8 adds, *"He will render to each one according to his works: to those who by patience in well-doing seek for glory and honor and immortality, he will give eternal life; but for those who are self-seeking and do not obey the truth, but obey unrighteousness, there will be wrath and fury."*

What is the result for those who are self-seeking and ignore the truth?

_____

_____

_____

<u>There is a Hell</u>

"I think hell's a real place where real people spend a real eternity."
Jerry Falwell

"There is no injustice in the grace of God. God is as just when He forgives a believer as when He casts a sinner into hell."
Charles Spurgeon

278

LESSON TWELVE HELL & HEAVEN

Do you agree or disagree with these quotes?

_____

_____

_____

Revelation 21:8 says, *"But as for the cowardly, the faithless, the detestable, as for murderers, the sexually immoral, sorcerers, idolaters, and all liars, their portion will be in the lake that burns with fire and sulfur, which is the second death."*

How is Hell described?

_____

_____

_____

Revelation 14:10-11
"He also will drink the wine of God's wrath, poured full strength into the cup of his anger, and he will be tormented with fire and sulfur in the presence of the holy angels and in the presence of the Lamb. And the smoke of their torment goes up forever and ever, and they have no rest, day or night, these worshipers of the beast and its image, and whoever receives the mark of its name."

What descriptions are given of Hell?

_____

_____

_____

"If we had more hell in the pulpit, we would have less hell in the pew." Billy Graham

279

LESSON TWELVE HELL & HEAVEN

Do you think Hell is discussed too much or not enough?

_____

_____

_____

Matthew 25:46 adds, *"And these will go away into eternal punishment, but the righteous into eternal life."*

How long is each destination?

_____

_____

_____

"I would rather go to heaven alone than go to hell in company."
R.A. Torrey

How would you reply to the person who says, "I do not care where I go because I will have friends in both places?"

_____

_____

_____

"Gehenna" is a Greek word translated as Hell. Charles C. Ryrie wrote that it is referencing a "refuse dump and a place of perpetual fire and loathsomeness, and the valley in Jerusalem illustrates the fire and awfulness of the lake of fire."

As a summary, how would you describe Hell?

_____

_____

_____

LESSON TWELVE HELL & HEAVEN

<u>There is a Heaven</u>

"To go to heaven, fully to enjoy God, is infinitely better than the most pleasant accommodations here." Jonathan Edwards

How do you view the worst day on earth compared to Hell, and the best day now compared to Heaven?

_____

_____

_____

Jesus says in John 14:1-3, *"Let not your hearts be troubled. Believe in God; believe also in me. In my Father's house are many rooms. If it were not so, would I have told you that I go to prepare a place for you? And if I go and prepare a place for you, I will come again and will take you to myself, that where I am you may be also."*

What does Jesus say about Heaven?

_____

_____

_____

In Luke 23:43, Jesus is talking to a thief on the cross, *"And he said to him, 'Truly, I say to you, today you will be with me in Paradise.'"*

What images come to mind with the word *"Paradise?"*

_____

_____

_____

LESSON TWELVE HELL & HEAVEN

Matthew 10:28 says, *"And do not fear those who kill the body but cannot kill the soul. Rather fear him who can destroy both soul and body in hell."*

Who is being referenced?

_____

_____

_____

Matthew 7:13-14 says, *"Enter by the narrow gate. For the gate is wide and the way is easy that leads to destruction, and those who enter by it are many. For the gate is narrow and the way is hard that leads to life, and those who find it are few."*

Does everyone go to Heaven? If not, the majority of people?

_____

_____

_____

Finally, Revelation 21:3-4 says, *"And I heard a loud voice from the throne saying, 'Behold, the dwelling place of God is with man. He will dwell with them, and they will be his people, and God himself will be with them as their God. He will wipe away every tear from their eyes, and death shall be no more, neither shall there be mourning, nor crying, nor pain anymore, for the former things have passed away.'"*

How is Heaven described?

_____

_____

_____

LESSON TWELVE HELL & HEAVEN

"For the Christian, heaven is where Jesus is. We do not need to speculate on what heaven will be like. It is enough to know that we will be forever with Him." William Barclay

LESSON TWELVE HELL & HEAVEN

REVELATION 14:10-11

HELL & HEAVEN, DEVOTION 1
Ryan Story | *Student Pastor*

We who know Jesus, have an amazing life ahead of us. All of us who have cried out for His grace and love have had our eternity changed. Regardless of how good or bad your life's circumstances have been, our eternity with Jesus is going to be indescribable! This is where you can cue the song by *MercyMe* "I Can Only Imagine." For those part of Christ's church, we all know the gift that is awaiting us one day. As amazing as that will be, there is always that sobering feeling in the back of my mind that screams, "What about those who do not?" Most estimate that 33% of the world would profess that they are Christ followers. Without even breaking that percentage down by who are truly following Christ, that means that only one in three people are going to be able to experience Heaven. Sixty Six percent of the world will be on the other side of eternity, Hell. By simple math, that means in just our lives, 5 billion people who currently live at the same time as us, are heading to an eternity that is without Christ Jesus.

Revelation 14:11 says, ***"And the smoke of their torment goes up forever and ever, and they have no rest, day or night, these worshipers of the beast and its image, and whoever receives the mark of its name."*** I cannot think of any worse description of a place to spend eternity. Sadly, we do not live our lives as if this is the eternal destination for the majority. Surely, if Christ-followers knew that people were destined for such a horrendous fate, we would step in and do something. Unfortunately, we all know we are too selfish, too self-involved, and too self-motivated to want to stop someone from this fate.

HELL & HEAVEN DEVOTION 1

In the book, *"When A Nation Forgets God,"* written by Dr. Erwin Lutzer, the author tells the following story from an eyewitness in Germany during the Holocaust:

"I lived in Germany during the Nazi Holocaust. I considered myself a Christian. We heard stories of what was happening to Jews, but we tried to distance ourselves from it because what could we do to stop it. A railroad track ran behind our small church, and each Sunday morning we could hear the whistle in the distance, and then the wheels coming over the tracks. We became disturbed when we heard the cries coming from the train as it passed. We realized that it was carrying Jews like cattle in the cars. Week after week the whistle would blow. We dreaded to hear the sound of those wheels because we knew that we would hear the cries of the Jews in route to a death camp. Their screams tormented us. We knew the time the train was coming, and when we heard the whistle blow, we began singing hymns. By the time the train came past our church, we were singing at the top of our voices. If we heard the screams, we sang more loudly and soon we heard them no more." Then the eyewitness shared with Pastor Lutzer, "Although years have passed, I still hear the train whistle in my sleep. God forgive me, forgive all of us who called ourselves Christians and yet did nothing to intervene."

How can a Christian sit idly as we know for a fact that our family members, neighbors, co-workers, and friends will spend eternity with no rest and their torment will be visible forever and ever? As Christians, we are not responsible for the outcome of them coming to know Jesus, the only thing we can be responsible for is opening our mouths and warning people about the fate that awaits them. Surely, if we knew where people would spend eternity, it would change the way we live our daily lives.

JOHN 3:16

HELL & HEAVEN, DEVOTION 2
James Clouse | *Student Pastor*

Before I became a pastor, I worked in sales. I worked in numerous hotels and worked my way from a front desk salesperson to manager of corporate sales. During that time, I would spend all my time and energy explaining why people needed to spend time and money at my hotel. It could be because it was more affordable, more comfortable, more perks, or because of the amazing service.

I am not a salesman anymore. God has called me to explain to people of the world where they should stay. As a pastor, I want to help you know where you should spend eternity. I have the perfect verse to help us understand what that means and how to get there.

"For God so loved the world, that he gave his only Son, that whoever believes in him should not perish but have eternal life." John 3:16

God gave His only son Jesus Christ, the Messiah of the world, to help us understand where to spend eternity. This is not an overnight business stay at a hotel. This is not a week somewhere on vacation. Where we go when we die is for the rest of time.

If you are one of those people who reads this and recognizes that you have a relationship with Jesus Christ and know where you are going when you die, fantastic! But I also realize that there are many that are going to read this that are not certain of where they are going when they die. Let me help you.

HELL & HEAVEN DEVOTION 2

Believe in what Jesus has done for us. The one who is without sin died for all those that have sinned. The one who knew no sin in His life gave up that life for us to have a relationship with God His Father. Those that do not recognize the truth of what Jesus did for us, die and spend eternity in Hell. Those amenities are horrible, the service is horrendous, and let me tell you it is not comfortable.

Romans 10:9 says, *"Because, if you confess with your mouth that Jesus is Lord and believe in your heart that God raised him from the dead, you will be saved."* If you are now one of those people reading this that wants that relationship with Jesus Christ, you need to believe it with all of your heart. Believe that Christ has died for you and your sins. Believe that Jesus not only died, but resurrected from the grave to defeat sin, death, and Hell. Come to another believer and tell them what you have done. Confess your relationship with a public display of baptism or tell your pastor.

Then you will be able to spend eternity with your Father where I do not need to sell the amenities or the service to you. You will be spending eternity with the Father. He is the one who loves us, created us, and gave up everything for us.

JOHN 3:36

HELL & HEAVEN, DEVOTION 3
Jayson Combs | *Family Pastor*

When you hear the words "eternal life," what immediately comes to your mind? John, the disciple, speaks of eternal life or everlasting life more than anyone else in the Bible. He uses it 18 times in the Gospel of John and six more times in the Epistle 1 John.

John states in John 3:36, *"Whoever believes in the Son has eternal life; whoever does not obey the Son shall not see life, but the wrath of God remains on him."* We see here as in other verses that eternal life is through no one else other than Jesus Christ. In John 6:68 (KJV), Peter answers Jesus, *"Lord, to whom shall we go? thou hast the words of eternal life".* Jesus tells us in John 10:28 (KJV), *"And I give unto them eternal life; and they shall never perish neither shall any one pluck them out of my hand".* Jesus is the way, the only way to eternal life.

I do believe there is some confusion though among believers when it comes to eternal life. In Daniel 12:2 it says, *"And many of those who sleep in the dust of the earth shall awake, some to everlasting life, and some to shame and everlasting contempt."* Life is everlasting no matter who you are. For some, it will be spent with the King of kings, for others under the wrath of God.

The other problematic view I see with many when it comes to eternal life is the focus on the destination. Yes, it is wonderful to know that Heaven is our home. It is exciting to think about Jesus who has gone and who is preparing a place for us. However, John tells us

HELL & HEAVEN DEVOTION 3

that eternal life is not just about the destination, it is about the trip. He writes in John 17:3, *"And this is eternal life, that they know you, the only true God, and Jesus Christ whom you have sent."* Eternal life is about a wonderful walk with Jesus that starts here on earth.

Are we there yet? Are we there yet? Are we there yet? When I was a child, our family vacation was always to Myrtle Beach. I can remember jumping into our great Pontiac 6000 and heading south. Flying was not an option, we drove. I can remember thinking how much I could not wait to get there so our vacation could begin. Thinking back on those amazing times makes me pause. I look back and think that vacation did not begin when we got there, it began when we left. I fondly remember those times in the car, the places that we stopped, and the adventures that we had. Now having a family of my own, we often have chosen to drive instead of flying.

Remember eternal life is not just the destination of Heaven. It is about the amazing walk with Jesus Christ.

REVELATION 21:8

HELL & HEAVEN, DEVOTION 4
Caleb Combs | *Gathering Pastor*

Eternity = Everlasting, infinity, time without end, timelessness, or in the words of Squints Palledorous, "FOR...EV...ER!" This is the most sobering concept in the Christian walk. The Bible is clear that if you have a personal relationship with Jesus Christ, you will spend eternity with Him. Eternity will be a place like no other, a place not built by the hands of man. It is a place with streets of gold, feasts celebrating the Lamb, and a house or mansion prepared specifically for me by the Master Builder Himself. Heaven will be a place where we celebrate what God has done for us and worship Him. I definitely can not say what every detail will look like, but I can tell you it will be a celebration like no other. I love this quote from Pastor John McArthur, "Heaven is a realm of unsurpassed joy, unfading glory, undiminished bliss, unlimited delights and unending pleasures." Sounds awesome!

The other side of the sobering concept is the realization of the alternative place of Heaven - Hell. It is a horrific place. The Bible tells us it is a place of darkness and death, where there will be weeping and gnashing of teeth. It is a place separate from the light of Jesus and absent of all hope. Revelation 21:8 describes it as a place that burns with fire and sulfur. Some may toss Hell and its description aside as imaginary, but it is a real place, just like Heaven. For those that never receive Christ as their Lord and Savior and never confess their sins, this is the place they will end up in for eternity. I do not say that with pride of happiness, but of fear and desperation knowing that millions of people around the world are heading for a future placed in Hell. I struggle even to type this, knowing that every second

HELL & HEAVEN DEVOTION 4

someone dies around the world, and they end up in one of two places, eternity with Christ in Heaven or eternity in Hell separated from Christ. There is no middle ground. There are no other options.

Revelation 21:8 tells us, *"But as for the cowardly, the faithless, the detestable, as for murderers, the sexually immoral, sorcerers, idolaters, and all liars, their portion will be in the lake that burns with fire and sulfur, which is the second death."*

Reading this verse, you may think, "Hey, I have lied. Does that mean I am going to Hell?" Or fill in your sin in place of lying and you and I are doomed to Hell. However, God does not look at us this way. When we are saved we become co-heirs, royal, holy, and children of the Almighty God. The Bible tells us that He has forgiven the sins of the past, present, and future. 2 Corinthians 5:17-18 tells us, *"Therefore, if anyone is in Christ, he is a new creation. The old has passed away; behold, the new has come. All this is from God, who through Christ reconciled us to himself and gave us the ministry of reconciliation."* That word reconciliation means to restore, and our relationship with Christ has been restored. We are in good standing with God, not by our works or deeds, but what Jesus did for us on the cross. When God looks at us, He sees that our debt has been paid through Christ, and counts us as righteous.

You may see yourself as a liar, coward, faithless, sexually immoral, or any of the other sins listed in Revelation 21:8, but if you are a child of God, that is not how He sees you. He views you through the lens of the blood of the Lamb that paid our debt; we are free and have hope for eternity with Him. If you know Jesus Christ as your Savior, you are a royal priesthood and do not let the enemy tell you differently. You have an assured hope in Heaven. If you do not know Christ or you are not sure, please take this time to cry out to God in your need for Him. If I can personally help you with this, please do

HELL & HEAVEN DEVOTION 4

not hesitate to ask. There is a Heaven and a Hell, and God has made a way for you to go to Heaven. Will you follow?

HELL & HEAVEN DEVOTION 4

ROMANS 2:6-8

HELL & HEAVEN, DEVOTION 5
Chuck Lindsey | *Reach Pastor*

"Who will render to each one according to his deeds: eternal life to those who by patient continuance in doing good seek for glory, honor, and immortality; but to those who are self-seeking and do not obey the truth, but obey unrighteousness—indignation and wrath, tribulation and anguish, on every soul of man who does evil..." Romans 2:6-9 (NKJV)

On July 8, 1741, American preacher Jonathan Edwards stood before the Enfield Connecticut congregation and read the words of what is now one of the most famous sermons in history. The sermon was entitled, *"Sinners in the hands of an angry God."* In it, Edwards vividly describes the severity of Hell, the immediate danger every mortal, sinful person is in, and the reality of eternity. This sermon found its mark and had a tremendous effect on the congregation that morning. Those present that day reported shrieks and screams from the unconverted as they realized their lost condition and the seriousness that they could at any moment enter eternity. The reality of an eternal Hell shook both the church there and the church across America for many years to come.

One of the most shocking pictures Edwards paints is that of eternity being unending. He said,

"It would be dreadful to suffer this fierceness and wrath of Almighty God one moment; but you must suffer it to all eternity. There will be no end to this exquisite, horrible misery. When you look forward,

HELL & HEAVEN DEVOTION 5

you shall see along forever a boundless duration before you, which will swallow up your thoughts, and amaze your soul. And you will absolutely despair of ever having any deliverance, any end, any mitigation, any rest at all. You will know certainly that you must wear out long ages, millions of millions of ages in wrestling with this almighty, merciless vengeance. And then when you have so done, when so many ages have actually been spent by you in this manner, you will know that all is but a point (moment) to what remains. So that your punishment will indeed be infinite."

Without question, this is why Jesus warned us so often against Hell. He spoke of it continually. Indeed, He came to rescue us from that dreadful place, to snatch us from those merciless and eternal flames. It is also why every apostle throughout the New Testament pleads with us to trust Christ, lest we send ourselves there.

In Romans 2:6-8, the Apostle Paul describes the difference between Heaven and Hell. He says that eternal life, blessing, and honor will be given to those who are born again. Eternal life is promised to those who have trusted in the work of Jesus Christ for the forgiveness of their sins. But to those who have not, to those who have (every single day of their lives) refused to trust Christ, rejected the truth and spent a lifetime serving themselves, they will suffer an eternity of the indignation and wrath of God. This will mean unending, unyielding tribulation and anguish. There will not be a moment of release from this. There will not be a moment of rest. There will not be a moment of relief. Hell is described as a worm that devours and never stops, and fires that are never extinguished.

Someone at this point might say, "How could God allow this?" But that is the wrong question. For God has done everything possible to keep a person from this. What more could He have done? He came; He died for our sins in our place on our cross. He went through the horrors of Hell and was raised from the dead to give us life. No, the question must never be, "How can God allow this?" The question can only be, "Why would anyone refuse Him?" "Why would anyone refuse His offer to rescue them?"

God does not send people to Hell. God sent His Son to keep us from Hell. People send themselves to Hell by refusing the Son and His sacrifice. This is something they must do every single day of their lives until they finally confirm it with their last breath.

For at the end of the day, eternity is where we get forever what we proved in our lives what we wanted most. Heaven belongs to those who love Him and have run to Him to be saved. It is those who want to spend eternity with the One who has rescued them, for He is their treasure.

Hell belongs to all those who all their lifetime refused and rejected Him. They will get forever what they proved by their lives they wanted most, existence apart from God.

HELL & HEAVEN DEVOTION 5

MATTHEW 25:46

HELL & HEAVEN, DEVOTION 6
Joshua Combs | *Lead Pastor*

"And these will go away into eternal punishment, but the righteous into eternal life."** Matthew 25:46

One of my favorite lines of poetry is from a Robert Frost poem entitled, *"The Road Not Taken."* At the end of this beautifully written word picture, he writes:

I shall be telling this with a sigh
Somewhere ages and ages hence:
Two roads diverged in a wood, and I –
I took the one less traveled by,
And that has made all the difference.

For whatever Frost's convictions were, this illustration of two clear, distinct paths was a consistent and clear theme in the teaching of Jesus. Nearly 2,000 years before Frost, Jesus, preaching on a Galilean hillside said, **"Enter by the narrow gate. For the gate is wide and the way is easy that leads to destruction, and those who enter by it are many. For the gate is narrow and the way is hard that leads to life, and those who find it are few"** (Matthew 7:13-14).

Two clear, unmistakably clear paths are laid before each person. The signs that label these two paths can be different: Christ or Satan, belief or unbelief, saved or unsaved, repentant or unrepentant, and the like. One road is wide and well-traveled, while the other is narrow and difficult.

HELL & HEAVEN DEVOTION 6

One day my wife, so brilliantly, described the road to me as a single lane path on the edge of a cliff, where we are often forced to walk sideways with our backs pressed against the cliff-side because the path has become so narrow. But like every road, these gates and paths of which Jesus spoke, have two very different destinations. The narrow gate and road lead to life, and the wide gate and road lead to destruction. One road leads to Heaven and the other Hell. Heaven is described as eternal life and joy in the presence of God. Hell is described as eternal suffering and sorrow away from the presence of God.

Every person has passed through one of these gates and is currently on one of these two roads. Which have you chosen? Have you passed through the gate of repentance and belief in Jesus Christ? If the answer is no, then quickly take the next exit, repent of your sin, believe in Jesus, and start walking the path of righteousness that leads to eternal life.

HELL & HEAVEN DEVOTION 6

OUR MISSION

Matthew 28:19-20: *"Go therefore and make disciples of all nations, baptizing them in the name of the Father and of the Son and of the Holy Spirit, teaching them to observe all that I have commanded you. And behold, I am with you always, to the end of the age."*

REACH

At The River Church, you will often hear the phrase, "we don't go to church, we are the Church." We believe that as God's people, our primary purpose and goal is to go out and make disciples of Jesus Christ. We encourage you to reach the world in your local communities.

GATHER

Weekend Gatherings at The River Church are all about Jesus, through singing, giving, serving, baptizing, taking the Lord's Supper, and participating in messages that are all about Jesus and bringing glory to Him. We know that when followers of Christ gather together in unity, it's not only a refresher it's bringing life-change.

GROW

Our Growth Communities are designed to mirror the early church in Acts as having "all things in common." They are smaller collections of believers who spend time together studying the word, knowing and caring for one another relationally, and learning to increase their commitment to Christ by holding one another accountable.

The River Church
8393 E. Holly Rd. Holly, MI 48442
theriverchurch.cc • info@theriverchurch.cc

BOOKS BY THE RIVER CHURCH

Made in the USA
Lexington, KY
09 September 2018